THE NEW YORK ABOLITIONISTS

Contributions
in American History
Series Editor:
STANLEY I. KUTLER
University of Wisconsin

THE NEW YORK ABOLITIONISTS

A Case Study of Political Radicalism

Gerald Sorin

*CONTRIBUTIONS IN
AMERICAN HISTORY*
Number 11

Greenwood Publishing Corporation
WESTPORT, CONNECTICUT

Library of Congress Catalog Card Number: 73–105981

SBN: 8371–3308–4

Greenwood Publishing Corporation
51 Riverside Avenue, Westport, Connecticut 06880
Greenwood Publishers Ltd.
42 Hanway Street, London, W.1., England

Printed in the United States of America

TO MY MOTHER AND FATHER

Contents

Contents

Preface

This study examines the social composition of abolitionist leadership in New York State from 1838 to 1845. More essentially, however, it attempts to test the validity of a general historical theory of political radicalism.

A significant number of social scientists, including historians, subscribe to what may generally be called the tension-reduction theory of political radicalism.[1] This theory holds that for radical reformers, such as abolitionists, the literal attainment of particular objectives, such as emancipation, is only a secondary consideration. The primary goal is to relieve through aggression, in the form of agitation, a profound psychological tension or frustration created by events, such as social dislocation, not necessarily related to the objects of reform, such as slavery.

Ironically, historians who subscribe to this theory are relying on a model of human behavior that is no longer accepted

[1] Many of these scholars have borrowed the concept from Harold Lasswell's *Psychopathology and Politics* (Chicago: University of Chicago Press, 1930), passim. For a detailed discussion of this point, see Gerald Sorin, "The Historical Theory of Political Radicalism: New York State Abolitionist Leaders as a Test Case" (Ph.D. diss., Columbia University, 1969), chapter 1.

as valid by the discipline of psychology from which it was lifted. Very few psychologists now claim that social tensions are the main source of frustration. Individuals are generally capable, it is thought, of reacting to new roles without experiencing any major frustrations. Also, different members of the same social class will perceive social challenges in different ways; many will experience no frustration at all.[2]

Moreover, even if we assume that social dislocation produces tension and frustration, there is great disagreement among psychologists about whether frustration automatically produces aggression. Some in fact have demonstrated that frustration more often produces anxiety, submission, dependency, or avoidance than aggression.[3] There is, thus, a growing and respectable group of psychologists who have shown that aggression is only one possible result of frustration. It is equally important that other psychologists have shown that frustration is only one possible source of aggression.[4]

Without denying tension reduction as a motive of certain kinds of human behavior, modern psychologists have demonstrated that it is possible, even in the area of aggressive behavior, to make room for another order of motivation—one set in a framework of cognition, rationality, maturity, and health.

We can admit the existence of consciousness and reason

2 A. H. Maslow, "Deprivation, Threat, and Frustration," in *Understanding Human Motivation*, ed. by C. L. Stacey and M. F. DeMartino (Cleveland: H. Allen, 1958); Saul Rosenzweig, "An Outline of Frustration Theory," in *Personality and Behavior Disorders*, ed. by J. McV. Hunt, vol. 1 (New York: Ronald Press, 1944).

3 Kenneth R. Wurtz, "Some Theory and Data Concerning the Attenuation of Aggression," *Journal of Abnormal and Social Psychology* 60 (January 1960): 134–136; J. P. Scott and Emil Fredericson, "The Causes of Fighting in Mice and Rats," *Physiological Zoology* 24 (October 1951): 280–308.

4 Leonard Berkowitz, *Aggression: A Social Psychological Analysis* (New York: McGraw-Hill Book Co., 1962), 29–36.

without reinstating the fiction of Rational Man. It is a false dichotomy to choose between man responding "instinctually" without benefit of consciousness and man rationally and consciously calculating his responses in a wholly undetermined context. For while psychologists and sociologists now claim that there is an undeniably rational component in men's opinions and actions, it is also claimed that that component is developed and operated in particular affective social environments.[5]

Thus behavior which appears to be psychologically determined may actually be in large part a response to the logic of the situation as seen by the actor—the actor's perspective having been influenced by a host of social variables. In short, a working assumption of this study has been that an historical analysis of radical reformers' actions and motives incorporating a sociological perspective may be more helpful than an analysis made primarily from a psychological perspective.

Specifically I have investigated and attempted to analyze, using sociological and psychological variables, New York State's abolitionist leaders. I have attempted to evolve a composite portrait of that group to determine whether it was more likely that these leaders were, in their militant behavior, responding "normally" to a challenge to their particular vision of America, or that these individuals experienced such abnormally intense economic, social, or personal frustration that they sought release from that frustration through agitation.

New York State is a good place for a study of abolitionist leadership. In 1835, almost half of the delegates to the Second

5 See M. Brewster Smith, Jerome S. Bruner, and Robert W. White, *Opinions and Personality* (New York: John Wiley, 1956); Silvan Tomkins, ed., *Affect, Cognition and Personality* (New York: Springer, 1965); Gordon W. Allport, "The Trend in Motivational Theory," *American Journal of Orthopsychiatry* 23 (January 1953): 107–119; Gardner Lindzey, ed., *Assessment of Human Motives* (New York: Holt, Rinehart & Winston, 1958).

Annual Meeting of the American Anti-Slavery Society were from the state of New York. By 1836 the executive committee of the National Society was unable to handle the magnitude of antislavery work going on in New York, and the State Society was formed. Furthermore, the Liberty party, organized in 1839, was essentially a New York State enterprise. And by 1844, of the approximately 62,000 Liberty voters in the nation, about 16,000 were in New York.

New York was also relatively representative of the northern states, containing at this time a wide variety of ethnic, religious, and socioeconomic groups.

Even if we cannot demonstrate the representative character of New York State during this period, it did contain approximately 14 percent of the American population. Thus, since the results of this study indicate that New York State abolitionist leaders were not abnormally frustrated people, agitating primarily to relieve tension, the general theory that radicals are motivated by a need to relieve themselves of personal psychological tension deserves to be seriously questioned.

Acknowledgments

I wish to thank Professor Lee Benson for providing the initial inspiration for this study and for his insights and criticism. I was fortunate to have Professor James P. Shenton's guidance in writing the doctoral dissertation from which this study emerged and wish to thank him for his perceptive suggestions. I am also indebted to my friend and colleague, Donald Roper, for his encouragement and criticism and to Carlton Mabee for a critical reading of the entire manuscript.

I appreciate the courtesies extended to me at the libraries of the following institutions: Manuscript Division at Syracuse University, New-York Historical Society, New York State Historical Association, New York Public Library, New York State Library, Oneida Historical Society, Buffalo and Erie County Public Library, and Cornell University. I am indebted to many local and county historians who supplied me with facts and source leads. My research was facilitated by a generous grant from the Joint Awards Council, University Awards Committee of the State University of New York Research Foundation. Finally, I thank my wife Myra, for without her support and encouragement at every stage I could not have produced this study.

THE NEW YORK ABOLITIONISTS

1

The Abolitionists and the Social Scientists

Theories of Motivation

THE New York abolitionist leaders were radical. They held ideas which were radical in substance—specifically, immediate emancipation and political and economic equality for blacks.[1] They led a social movement and participated in agitation for direct action which would eventuate in freedom for blacks and a society of racial brotherhood; and ultimately they experienced a total commitment to abolitionism.

The historians who have borrowed from psychology the tension-reduction theory of radical reform are primarily concerned with radicals who agitate. Agitation is seen as a form of aggression, an aggression induced by frustration. David Donald, for example, sees the abolitionist leaders as victims of

---

[1] This was an extreme doctrine. It meant the liquidation of millions of dollars worth of chattel and the injection of millions of new untutored citizens into a society whose existing institutions, customs, and social structure would feel widespread effect.

3

an alleged industrial revolution; as a "displaced class in American society," a former elite group frustrated by a "drastic dislocation of northern society," participating in agitation because it "allowed the only chance for personal and social self-fulfillment." The abolitionist leaders, for Donald, were men and women with lowered status suffering from a "profound social and psychological dislocation."[2] Agitation for the abolition of slavery, according to a recent article in the *Journal of Southern History,* "fulfilled certain needs and alleviated vague frustrations."[3]

Many historians have characterized their work on abolitionist leaders with similar themes referring to the reformers' motivation as a function of "maladjustments," "desire for martyrdom," the "easing of guilt," "psychic forces clamoring for expression," and as an "outgrowth of desperate inner needs."[4] It is relatively easy to document the fact that in

2 David Donald, "Toward a Reconsideration of Abolitionists," *Lincoln Reconsidered* (New York: Alfred Knopf, 1956), pp. 28–36. In a collective analysis of America's radical right that appeared a year before Donald's book, a number of social scientists made use of the concept of status frustration to describe the motivation of their subjects. Status dislocation and its ensuing frustrations, according to Seymour Lipset, can push the individual into agitational politics which permits the discharging of aggression without ever proposing a clear-cut solution. Seymour Lipset, "Sources of the 'Radical Right,'" in *New American Right,* ed. by Daniel Bell (New York: Criterion Books, 1955), pp. 167–168.

3 Anne C. Loveland, "Evangelicalism and 'Immediate Emancipation' in American Antislavery Thought," *Journal of Southern History* 32 (May 1966): 180.

4 See Avery Craven, *The Coming of the Civil War* (New York: Charles Scribner's Sons, 1942), pp. 117–118; W. H. and Jane H. Pease, "Antislavery Ambivalence: Immediatism, Expediency and Race," *American Quarterly* 17 (Winter 1965): 693–695; Eliza Wigham, *The Anti-Slavery Cause in America and Its Martyrs* (London: A. W. Bennett, 1863); Hazel C. Wolf, *On Freedom's Altar: The Martyr Complex in the Abolition Movement* (Madison: University of Wisconsin Press, 1952); Stanley Elkins, *Slavery: A Problem in American Institutional and Intellectual Life* (Chicago: University of Chicago Press, 1959); George F. Milton, *Eve of Conflict: Stephen A. Douglas and the Needless War* (New York: Houghton

attempting to explain the motivations of abolitionist leaders, historians, until very recently, have generally emphasized tension reduction, i.e., that the radical agitator's opinions and actions are not much more than a function of his own psychic needs or conflicts.[5] In the case of the abolitionist leaders in New York, agitation as a means appears to have grown out of the specific social situation in which the reformers found themselves. Those New Yorkers who became abolitionist leaders in the 1830s were intensely and actively religious people. And in the context of the evangelical revivalism of the 1820s and 1830s which indicted slavery as a sin, it is highly likely, given the evidence that will follow, that many of them were strongly attracted to the idea of abolitionism.

Holding a radical idea which they wished to see implemented, abolitionists were, however, surrounded by intransigence and overt hostility. It is possible, thus, to view the action abolitionists took as a direct and logical response to the situation. For, as modern psychology has demonstrated, an aggressive posture and militant behavior may be a perfectly normal reaction to a challenge.[6] The existence of slavery, the

Mifflin, 1934); Fawn M. Brodie, *Thaddeus Stevens* (New York: W. W. Norton, 1959), p. 10. See also Charles C. Cole, *The Social Ideas of the Northern Evangelists, 1826–1860* (New York: Columbia University Press, 1954), pp. 207–220; Walter M. Merrill, *Against Wind and Tide* (Cambridge: Harvard University Press, 1963), p. 40; David Donald, *Charles Sumner and the Coming of the Civil War* (New York: Alfred A. Knopf, 1961).

[5] For a detailed documentation, see Martin Duberman, "Abolitionists and Psychology," *Antislavery Vanguard* (Princeton: Princeton University Press, 1965); Betty Fladeland, "Who Were the Abolitionists?," *Journal of Negro History* 49 (April 1964): 99–115; Fawn Brodie, "Who Defends the Abolitionist?" *Antislavery Vanguard;* Bertram Wyatt-Brown, "Abolitionism: Its Meaning for Contemporary American Reform," *Midwest Quarterly* 8 (October 1966): 53.

[6] Rudolf Heberle, *Social Movements* (New York: Appleton-Century-Crofts, 1951), p. 109.

complacency of Americans in regard to the "peculiar institution," and the resistance to reform of the system constituted
a challenge to the vision of the abolitionists of what America
should be.

By assuming that social dislocation and ensuing frustration
or tension produced abolitionism, a number of historians have
approached the basic questions about social and political
movements from a very narrow psychological viewpoint.
Moreover, the psychological bases of the assumption have been
disproved or at least disputed by recent work in psychology.

In the last decade, revision has begun among psychologists
and sociologists of the older behaviorist model of human conduct. Behaviorists had emphasized "tension reduction" as the
main goal of men's thoughts and actions. Individuals were
motivated, it was thought, by "a state of tenseness that leads us
to seek equilibrium, rest, adjustment, satisfaction or homeo-
stasis. From this point of view personality is nothing more
than our habitual modes of reducing tension."[7] Now a new
framework for the study of behavior is being evolved which
includes consciousness and which makes room for rationality
and for complex motives involving abstract ideas such as
freedom, love, and equality, as well as "drives."

Men, according to the recent literature, are not only re-
covering their minds, but also their hearts and their feelings.[8]
All of this makes possible a dynamic as opposed to a merely
instinctive life. Men can be reasoning organisms capable of
decisions and choice.

As early as 1951, before the current revision had begun, the
political sociologist, Rudolf Heberle, wrote that the psycho-
pathological explanation of the motivation of radicals was unsatisfactory. Although Heberle considered it legitimate to ask,

[7] Gordon Allport, *Becoming: Basic Considerations for a Psychology of
Personality* (New Haven: Yale University Press, 1955), pp. 48–49.
[8] Silvan Tomkins, ed., *Affect, Cognition and Personality* (New York:
Springer, 1965), p. vii.

"To what extent are neurotic and psychopathic individuals more frequently found in social movements than among the non-participating population,"[9] he believes the tension-reduction explanation fails because, among other reasons, it does not make a distinction between "idealists" and "activists." The great majority of the leaders and of the rank and file in radical, militant movements, Heberle writes, are not political activists who find fulfillment in political action as such; rather, "they are typically idealists in the sense that they are unshakably convinced of the righteousness of their cause, of the validity of their philosophy, and the goodness of their goals."[10] For Heberle, it is from this conviction "which often assumes a quasi-religious quality,"[11] that political movements derive their vitality and not from, as the tension-reduction theory would have it, "the displacement of private affects upon public objects."[12]

The methodological mistake of psychoanalytic explanations, Heberle writes, consists "in the direct, unmodified application of categories of personality psychology to the analysis and characterization of highly complex and flexible social groups."[13] It is extremely difficult to determine the exact frequency of certain motives among a multitude of individuals; the very complexity of motives makes any accurate determination difficult. Furthermore, "most men will be motivated not in one way or the other but by a combination of motives, and any movement will contain quite a variety of differently motivated adherents or followers."[14]

Any social movement, Heberle continues, such as abolition-

9 Heberle, *Social Movements*, p. 104. Heberle cites Harold Lasswell among other social scientists.
10 Ibid., p. 116.
11 Ibid.
12 Harold Lasswell, *Psychopathology and Politics* (Chicago: University of Chicago Press, 1930), p. 183.
13 Heberle, *Social Movements*, p. 108.
14 Ibid., p. 99.

ism, which rebels against existing social institutions will attract "neurotic, maladjusted, unbalanced, or psychopathic
personalities."[15] But, these types are "activists" and seem to
be attracted not so much by the ideas as by the promise of
action, and "by the sense of oneness, of belonging, which ap-
peases their feelings of insecurity, of helplessness, of isolation."[16] The majority of those attracted, however, are
"idealists" attracted "by the ideals of the movement," and are
only secondarily, if at all, "activists"—that is, primarily "concerned with the action."[17] Not denying the possible contributions of personality analysis toward the understanding of social
behavior, Heberle maintains "that the immediate and significant causes" of a social movement "will not be found in
the condition of the leaders' minds or in the neuroses of their
followers."[18]

Psychologist Gordon W. Allport not only puts less emphasis
on "tension reduction" as a component in the explanation of
human motivation, but, he wrote, the very mark of maturity
"seems to be the range and extent of one's feeling of self-
involvement in abstract ideals,"[19] and that mature behavior
may aim at distant goals the achievement of which can be
gained only *by maintaining tension.*[20]

Distant-goal seeking and involvement in abstract ideals was
a significant element in the behavior of the abolitionists.
Psychologist Silvan Tomkins describes this seeking and involvement as "resonance":

15 Ibid., p. 113.
16 Ibid.
17 Ibid., p. 114. Heberle came to this conclusion on the basis of evidence he gathered from social movements and political parties for a study
of the psychology of such phenomena.
18 Herberle, *Social Movements,* p. 111; M. Brewster Smith, "Opinions,
Personality and Political Behavior," *American Political Science Review* 52
(March 1959): 3.
19 Allport, *Becoming,* p. 45.
20 Ibid., pp. 65–68.

By resonance we mean the engagement of feeling and thought by any organized ideology or social movement. The fit between the individual's own loosely organized ideas and feelings . . . and the more tightly organized ideology or social movement need not be a very close one to induce resonance.[21]

The plight of the black slave in nineteenth century America, Tomkins explains, induced resonance in men for many reasons:

Some men resonated to abolitionism because slavery violated their Christian faith; others because of a general sympathy for the underdog; others because of belief in the perfectibility of man; others because of a belief in the democratic assertion of the equal rights of all men, or in individualism. . . .[22]

Tomkins traces the development of the original resonance through several stages to final "commitment." Resonance can be built in through a simple process—a loving father dedicated to the salvation of others might provide a model which predisposed the son to resonate to movements based on public service or helping others, such as abolitionism. At a given point, risk is ventured on behalf of those who need to be helped, and as a consequence of risk taken there is punishment and suffering; as a consequence of these, attraction to the original idea, identification with the oppressed, and hostility toward the oppressor and those who remain uncommitted increases, and as a result there is imbued an increasing willing-

[21] Silvan Tomkins, "The Psychology of Commitment: The Constructive Role of Violence and Suffering for the Individual and for his Society," in *Antislavery Vanguard*, p. 280.

[22] Ibid., p. 281. It is in the context of the 1830s and 1840s in America that most of the concepts Tomkins mentions above—democracy, individualism, perfectibility—come to be greatly emphasized. Thus abolitionism, for many, could be a response to the logic of the situation—as seen by the actor. This idea will be developed at greater length in chapters 2–4.

ness to take even greater risks. This cycle repeats itself, cumu-
latively deepening commitment until it reaches a "point of
no return."[23]

In a significant note, Tomkins states that "the pathway from
early resonance to final commitment is not necessarily without
internal conflict." In the men he studied, "each suffered doubt
at some point whether to give himself completely to abolitionism as a way of life."[24] Thus they were not necessarily impelled
to commit themselves to radical reform by the need to reduce
personal tensions or the unconscious tensions of social dislocation, but may have come to that commitment deliberately,
after reflection. The only frustration that seems relevant here
is that encountered *after* the original "risk" has been taken,
rather than that suffered prior to one's involvement in reform.

The work of psychologists Allport and Tomkins suggests
that concern and commitment and radical action need not be
aberrations at all. Erich Fromm, in *The Sane Society*, spells
out the implications of this kind of reasoning and suggests
that "society as a whole may be lacking in sanity,"[25] and that
society's rebels may be genuinely attempting to correct the
folie à millions of a given social order.[26] It is naively assumed,
Fromm writes, "that the fact that the majority of people share
certain ideas or feelings proves the validity of these ideas and
feelings; nothing is farther from the truth."[27] The fact that a
majority of people "share the same form of mental pathology
does not make these people sane."[28]

23 Ibid., passim.

24 Ibid., p. 292.

25 Erich Fromm, *The Sane Society* (New York: Holt, Rinehart, and
Winston, 1960), p. 8.

26 Ibid., p. 15. See also in this regard, Erich Fromm, "The Revolutionary
Character," *The Dogma of Christ* (New York: Holt, Rinehart, and Winston, 1963).

27 Ibid.

28 Ibid.

Despite the fact that many psychiatrists and psychologists "hold that the problem of mental health in a society is only that of the number of 'unadjusted' individuals, and not that of a possible unadjustment of the culture itself,"[29] Fromm says "the criterion of mental health is not one of individual adjustment to a given social order," but "must be defined in terms of the adjustment of society to the needs of man."[30] Otherwise, "social psychology instead of being a tool for the criticism of society," becomes "the apologist for the status quo."[31]

Within the sociopsychological framework set up by Fromm, it is possible to ask, as Martin Duberman does, "whether the abolitionists, in insisting that slavery be ended, were indeed those men of their generation furthest removed from reality, or whether that description should be reserved for those Northerners who remained indifferent to the institution, and those Southerners who defended it as a 'positive good.' "[32]

Taken together, the works of Fromm, Allport, Tomkins, and Heberle imply that critics of society may very well be sincere idealists with greater convictions about social justice, with greater "integrity and sensitivity than the majority," and

29 Ibid., p. 8.
30 Ibid., pp. 14, 72.
31 Ibid., p. 73.
32 Duberman, "Northern Response to the Antislavery Movement," *Antislavery Vanguard*, pp. 412–413. In this regard, it is instructive to note the results of the research of Herbert McClosky, carried out through the Laboratory for Research in Social Relations, University of Minnesota: "Conservatism . . . appears to be far more characteristic of social isolates, of people . . . who suffer personal disgruntlement and frustration. . . . Poorly integrated psychologically, anxious, often perceiving themselves as inadequate, and subject to excessive feelings of guilt, they seem inclined to project onto others the traits they most dislike or fear in themselves." ("Conservatism and Personality," *American Political Science Review* 52 [March 1958]: 37–38). Similar findings are reported in Richard S. Crutchfield, "Conformity and Character," *American Psychologist* 10 (1955): 191–198.

who happen to be strong enough "to live soundly 'against the stream.' "[33] Some historians, writing about abolitionism, have characterized their respective works with similar themes.

For Gilbert Hobbs Barnes, in *Anti-Slavery Impulse* (1933), and Whitney Cross, in *Burned-Over District* (1950), the abolitionists were religious zealots to whom social reforms symbolized stepping-stones toward the millennium. Both historians point to the dynamic impact of the revivalism of Charles G. Finney as the primary impulse for abolitionism, and would agree with Heberle that the majority of abolitionist leaders were "quasi-religious" idealists "unshakably convinced of the righteousness of their cause . . . the goodness of their goals."[34]

In every community that Finney invaded, he left groups of young men "overflowing with benevolence for unsaved mankind."[35] To these newborn converts "fresh from the ardor of revival, social ills seemed easily curable, and dreams of reform were future realities."[36]

Cross believes that one of the manifestations of the religious ultraism described by Barnes was the intensification of the demand in the 1830s for immediate emancipation.[37] This tremendous influence of Finney's revivals, "though it long survived, came primarily from the great campaigns of 1826 and 1831, more particularly from the latter."[38] Religious ultraism was not only the impulse for immediate abolitionism, Cross writes; it generally engendered a strong sense of social

---

[33] Fromm, *The Sane Society*, p. 15.

[34] Heberle, *Social Movements*, p. 116.

[35] Gilbert Hobbs Barnes, *Antislavery Impulse: 1830–1844* (New York: D. Appleton-Century Co., Inc., 1933), p. 12.

[36] Ibid., p. 16.

[37] Whitney R. Cross, *The Burned-Over District: The Social and Intellectual History of Enthusiastic Religion in Western New York, 1800–1850* (Ithaca: Cornell University Press, 1950), p. 217. Even Cross, who labels the religious enthusiasts as vital and courageous, suggests that they were "misled," and were involved in a futile expenditure of energy, p. 356.

[38] Ibid., p. 156.

justice and therefore was "the precedent condition to all ensuing crusades."[39]

Between 1964 and 1966 four articles appeared which "defend" the abolitionist leaders of the nineteenth century. Betty
Fladeland and Martin Duberman have written in separate
pieces that while it is true that much of abolitionist propaganda was directed at the emotions, and that the "evangelical
rhetoric of the movement, with its thunderous emphasis on
sin and retribution, can sound downright 'queer' (and thus
'neurotic') to the 20th century skeptic,"[40] these "tendencies
were not the monopoly of abolitionists. . . . The historical
context was one of faddist panaceas and Utopian experi-
mentation."[41]

Duberman goes on to say that "actually, behavioral patterns
for many abolitionists do *not* seem notably eccentric." And in
any case, he asks, "Could any verbal protest have been too
strong against holding fellow human beings as property?"[42]

In an article that appeared in *Antislavery Vanguard* along
with Duberman's, Fawn Brodie asks why it is in our recent
histories that Charles Sumner's speeches against slavery are
analyzed and found to be pure rant and in deplorable taste
at the same time that the proslavery speeches of someone
like Senator Andrew P. Butler generally go undissected and
uncriticized; why it is that the "hidden motives" of Senator
Butler and Congressman Preston Brooks who beat Sumner
into insensibility in the Senate chamber remain inviolate,
while historians search the abolitionist Sumner's motives for
arrogance, sexual impotence, or desire for martyrdom?[43]

[39] Ibid., pp. 197, 208. For a similar, somewhat more recent view, see
John L. Thomas, "Antislavery and Utopia," in *Antislavery Vanguard*,
pp. 240–269.
[40] Duberman, "Northern Response to the Antislavery Movement," p. 408.
[41] Fladeland, "Who Were the Abolitionists?", p. 106.
[42] Duberman, "Northern Response to the Antislavery Movement," pp.
409, 411.
[43] Brodie, "Who Defends the Abolitionist?", pp. 53–54.

Rather than finding evidence of instability and neuroses among the abolitionist leaders, Bertram Wyatt-Brown writes that "it could be said that they were one of the happiest sets of reformers in American history."[44] Wyatt-Brown advises his readers not to pity the abolitionists' psychological problems, but to appreciate their significant contribution to our reform tradition.[45]

The best and most direct "defense" of militant abolitionism as a logical and appropriate response to an evil situation, is still David Brion Davis's "The Emergence of Immediatism in British and American Antislavery Thought."[46] The majority of the abolitionist leaders in the 1830s, according to Davis, realized that instant and unconditional liberation of the slaves would be madness, but felt a "direct intuitive consciousness of the sinfulness of slavery, and a sincere personal commitment"[47] to demand an "immediate beginning of direct action that would eventuate in general emancipation."[48]

[44] Wyatt-Brown, "Abolitionism: Its Meaning for Contemporary American Reform," p. 53.

[45] Ibid., p. 55. For other works which take nonhostile positions toward the abolitionists see: Richard Hofstadter, "Wendell Phillips," *American Political Tradition* (New York: Alfred A. Knopf, 1948); John Hope Franklin, *From Slavery to Freedom* (New York: Alfred A. Knopf, 1947); Russel B. Nye, *Fettered Freedom* (East Lansing: Michigan State University Press, 1949); Ralph Korngold, *Two Friends of Man: William Lloyd Garrison and Wendell Phillips* (Boston: Little Brown, 1950); Benjamin Thomas, *Theodore Weld* (New Brunswick: Rutgers University Press, 1950); Betty Fladeland, *James G. Birney* (Ithaca: Cornell University Press, 1955); Oscar Sherwin, *Prophet of Liberty* (New York: Bookman Associates, 1956); Irving Bartlett, *Wendell Phillips* (Boston: Beacon Press, 1961); Dwight Dumond, *Antislavery: The Crusade for Freedom in America* (Ann Arbor: University of Michigan Press, 1961); Bertram Wyatt-Brown, *Lewis Tappan and the Evangelical War Against Slavery* (Cleveland: Case Western Reserve University Press, 1969); Aileen S. Kraditor, *Means and Ends in American Abolitionism* (New York: Pantheon, 1968); Benjamin Quarles, *Black Abolitionists* (New York: Oxford University Press, 1969).

[46] David B. Davis, "The Emergence of Immediatism in British and American Antislavery Thought," *Mississippi Valley Historical Review* 49 (September 1962): 209–230.

[47] Ibid., p. 209.   [48] Ibid., p. 213.

In one sense, Davis writes, immediatism was a logical culmination of earlier antislavery movements and was "brought on by the failure of less direct plans for abolition."[49] The British Anti-Slavery Society was officially gradualist until 1831, but was becoming "increasingly impatient over the diffidence of the government,"[50] and although still cautious, urged direct Parliamentary intervention.

When the British government finally revealed its plan

> for gradual and compensated emancipation the Anti-Slavery Society committed itself to vigorous and aggressive opposition. But once the law had been passed, the antislavery leaders concluded that they had done as well as possible and that their defeat had actually been a spectacular victory. They had achieved their primary object, which was to induce the people to support a tangible act that could be interpreted as purging the nation of collective guilt and proving the moral power of individual conscience.[51]

The British abolitionists had grown tired of "irrelevant palliatives," and agitated about a social change which in the end *was* substantially affected. "The American anti-slavery organization" soon "absorbed some of this sense of urgency and mistrust of palliatives."[52] And in 1831 a "new generation of American reformers adopted the principle of immediatism," which "had had a long and parallel development"[53] in England and America.

To the American and British abolitionist leaders, however, emancipation was not simply "an objective matter of social or political expediency, but a subjective act of purification and a casting off of sin."[54] A sense of moral urgency and fear of

49 Ibid., p. 227.
50 Ibid., p. 219.
51 Ibid., p. 222.
52 Ibid.
53 Ibid., p. 225.
54 Ibid., p. 212.

divine retribution persisted in antislavery thought. From the evangelical revivals of this period, the abolitionist derived a strong sense of "personal commitment to make no compromise with sin."[55]

Even if the slaveholder rejected the new convert's appeal to his unrepented conscience, the latter "was at least assured of his own freedom from guilt."[56] But the abolitionist did fervently hope that people could be convinced that slavery was wrong, that they could be convinced that his moral and political demands bore relevance to social needs, and that they could be convinced to force "governments to take care of the details."[57]

Davis demonstrates that immediate abolitionism was a shift in social and political strategy due to the failure of earlier, more gradual plans, and symptomatic of a shift toward accepting personal responsibility for the sin of slavery, a responsibility engendered by evangelical revivals. He shows that the militant agitation involved in the movement was not enough for the abolitionist leader, whose valid discontent would not be relieved until he could substantially affect the society in which he lived by helping God eliminate a concrete sin, and "triumph over all that was mean and selfish and worldly."[58]

The abolitionist sought to accomplish this through an upsurge of moral action on the part of the public; this was possible for him because he believed "that ideas held with sufficient intensity can be transformed into irresistible moral action."[59] Davis's claims warrant placing the abolitionist lead-

---

[55] Ibid., p. 228. There are definite links, writes Davis, "between immediate emancipation and a religious sense of immediate justification and presence of the divine spirit that can be traced through the early spiritual religions to the Quakers, Methodists, and evangelical revivals."
[56] Ibid.
[57] Ibid., p. 227.
[58] Ibid., p. 228.
[59] Ibid., p. 230.

ers into Heberle's category of "idealists" rather than of "activists."[60] For Davis argues that the leaders were concerned primarily with the goals of the movement and only secondarily with the action—that they were responding appropriately to an evil situation which challenged their vision of a "free and Christian society."[61]

The Davis thesis, making effective use of the works of Barnes and Cross, and reflecting, consciously or otherwise, the sociopsychological outlooks of Heberle, Fromm, and Allport (suggesting that the very definition of maturity may be the ability to commit oneself to and act to fulfill abstract ideals), constitutes, in my view, a comprehensive counter-hypothesis to the thesis suggested by David Donald's, Stanley Elkins's, and other historians' application of tension-reduction motivation theory to the abolitionist movement. The test for the validity of any approach is not theoretical, of course, but empirical. In this case, the unsoundness of the sociological and psychological theories which underlie the assumption that social tensions produced abolitionism becomes obvious after an examination of the types of men who became abolitionists.

Research Design and Method

The new psychology suggests that commitment need not be a symptom of personality disturbance. It is equally possible that committing oneself to the achievement of distant goals based on abstract ideals is a symptom of maturity and health. This is not to say that the majority of abolitionists protested out of mature motives, but given the new motivational theory

---

60 Heberle, *Social Movements,* p. 116.
61 Davis, "Emergence of Immediatism," p. 229.

this is at least as possible as the abolitionists agitating to relieve themselves of frustration.

It takes the skill of a competent psychiatrist to determine whether attitudes, behavior, and reactions of certain groups are due to frustration or not. It is also difficult to determine whether unusual frustration, i.e., more than the normal frustration inherent in human existence, has been experienced by individual members of the group. The question of disturbance or maturity as motive is even more difficult to test for the historian than for the psychologist. The subjects are dead, and any analysis must be attempted on the basis of fragmentary materials.

Forewarned, I hope at least to make a beginning in the attempt to determine whether abolitionist leaders in New York were primarily individuals who experienced such abnormally intense economic, social or personal frustration, that it was possible for them to seek release from that frustration through agitation, or whether these leaders suffered no more or different frustration than that which human beings tend to experience, and were therefore, in their militant behavior, simply responding normally to a challenge to their particular vision of America. In short, I have tried to determine whether the abolitionist leaders generally fit Heberle's category of "activists" attracted to the movement by its promise of action, or generally were "idealists" attracted primarily by the ideals and goals of the movement.

I chose 1838–1845 for my study inasmuch as it was during these years that the Liberty party was set up in New York State. Liberty men were originally moral suasion abolitionists who became convinced that their efforts for reform regarding the free Negro and abolition would fail unless made in the political arena.[62] Leaders of the Liberty party discouraged

[62] Alice Henderson, "History of the New York State Antislavery Society" (Ph.D. diss., University of Michigan, 1963), passim; John Hendricks, "History of the Liberty Party in New York State, 1840–1848" (Ph.D. diss.,

but undaunted by initial failure in the elections of 1840, spent the years prior to the next presidential election building and extending their organization.[63] They ran candidates during these years for local and state offices, and this enabled me to rank abolitionist leaders in order of influence, something much harder to do prior to the organization of the party.[64]

The candidates run by the Liberty party cared *intensely* enough about abolishing the "peculiar institution" to desert their former parties. Intensity here must be emphasized, for to switch parties in mid-nineteenth century America meant overcoming strong counterpressures regarding fidelity and meant risking a charge of something akin to treason.[65]

One of the criteria I used for selecting individuals for investigation, however, was that they had to have been interested in antislavery as a moral question before 1835–1836. This not only cleared each subject selected of the suspicion of being "politically" motivated; it also distinguished the abolitionists as a group from their milder cousins, the antislavery people. This latter group of what in modern times might be called

---

Fordham University, 1958), passim; Lee Benson, *The Concept of Jacksonian Democracy: New York as a Test Case* (Princeton: Princeton University Press, 1961), pp. 110–114.

63 Benson, *Concept of Jacksonian Democracy*, p. 113.

64 *Albany Patriot*, ed., James C. Jackson, 5 October 1842–24 October 1843; *Emancipator*, ed., Joshua Leavitt, 1840–1844; *Friend of Man*, ed., William Goodell, 1840–1841; *Liberty Press*, ed., James C. Jackson, extant issues 1843–1844. In addition the voters for the party in New York grew from approximately 2,800 to 16,000 in 1844. The impression one gets from the antislavery literature and newspapers is that this growth was generally within abolitionist ranks. Originally many members of the Anti-Slavery Society did not support the plans for political action, especially the establishment of an independent party. These members had expressed feelings about other issues and were often, at first, quite unwilling to cross party lines. Yet by late 1841 the line between the New York State Anti-Slavery Society and the Liberty party was becoming blurred.

65 Benson, *Concept of Jacksonian Democracy*, p. 64ff.

"fellow travelers" grew rapidly in New York and in the nation generally after 1835 because of the increasing indifference by the "slave power" and the mob to the long boasted hereditary rights of freedom of speech and the liberty of the press. The "gag" rules, sponsored by southern representatives in Congress, effectively closing off debate on slavery, which were a virtual if not a technical violation of the First Amendment,[66] and the proslavery interest's "interference" in the previously sacrosanct United States mails during 1835–1836 to prevent circulation of abolitionist literature aroused more interest in antislavery than the abolitionists could have in many years.[67] The same is true of mob action against abolitionists—their persons, their property, and their meetings—which occurred during 1835–1836, especially in New York State.[68]

These fellow travelers were attracted to antislavery during these years primarily because a new issue was engendered— the civil liberties of white American citizens.[69] It is still possible, of course, that the men who joined the abolitionists after 1836 were not fellow travelers but true converts.[70] These were investigated closely to see whether it was civil liberties

[66] James M. McPherson, "Fight Against the Gag Rule: Joshua Leavitt and Anti-Slavery Insurgency in the Whig Party, 1839–42," *Journal of Negro History* 48 (July 1963): 177–195.

[67] Nye, *Fettered Freedom*, passim.

[68] Samuel Bemis, *John Quincy Adams and the Union* (New York: Alfred A. Knopf, 1956); *Emancipator*, 1835–1836; *Friend of Man*, 1836.

[69] "The violence inflicted on the early abolitionists and the suffering they endured led others to take up their cause; it is here that we see the collective influence of these men on their society" (Tomkins, "The Psychology of Commitment," p. 292).

[70] Silvan Tomkins explains that "in a democratic society, based on belief in individualism and egalitarianism, it is possible to arouse vicarious distress, shame, fear, or sympathy for a victim and anger or contempt for an aggressor. As a by-product, the ideas of the victim [abolitionism] will then tend to become more influential than before such an attack" (Ibid., p. 295).

"Such violence and suffering can, in a democratic society arouse in outside observers *equally intense feeling* [italics added]" (Ibid.)

they were out to protect, i.e., the rights of the white man, or whether it was interest in black slaves and free Negroes which engaged them.

In any case, the use of the 1836 criterion enabled me to select not only prominent Liberty leaders, but men who were definitely abolitionists. This particular criterion, however, was applied at a later stage in the process of selection; the first step in my undertaking, of course, was to identify New York State antislavery leaders.

I used New York antislavery and nonantislavery sources and national antislavery sources. I turned first to the primary New York antislavery source, the official newspapers of the New York State Anti-Slavery Society and of the Liberty party—the *Emancipator,* the *Friend of Man,* the *Liberty Press,* and the *Albany Patriot.* I systematically read the issues from 1838 to 1845 and noted the names of those who were nominated for office on the Liberty ticket; those who held important posts within the party machinery itself: convention and committee chairmen, delegates, district leaders, and so on; state and local antislavery society executives; and those who did not hold office but seemed generally influential because their names appeared continuously from week to week.

I read the reports of the New York State Anti-Slavery Society and the *Colored American* and gleaned more names of of those who held executive positions within the society.

Having gathered six hundred names from New York antislavery sources, I then selected the four hundred most prominent by means of the following point system: a nominee for office on the state or national level received more points than a party officer of corresponding level because the former, necessarily exposed to greater numbers of people during campaigns and the like, was generally more influential in the role of molding public opinion, had greater opportunity to agitate, and presumably was judged more influential by men who controlled the nominations. The president of the New York State Anti-Slavery Society was included in the highest rank because he was the leader of an organization which contained virtually the entire Liberty party in addition to most of New York's abolitionists who were unaffiliated with the Liberty party.

Party officers on the state level were granted more points than officers of corresponding rank in abolitionist societies on the county level, again because of greater exposure. However, an officer of an antislavery society on the county level received more credit than a party officer on the same level, because the former had influence over nonpolitical abolitionists as well as political ones.

A committee chairman at a convention (e.g., county level) received equal points with a committee member or delegate at one higher level (e.g., state), because of the more influential nature of the chairman's job. Nonpresidential executives of antislavery societies on local levels were rated relatively low because their positions were largely honorary.

6 points: 1) Nominee for Congress
2) President of N.Y.S. Anti-Slavery Society

5 points: Nominee for State Legislature

4 points: State Party Convention Chairman

3 points: 1) President of County Antislavery Society
2) National Convention Delegate
3) State Convention Committee Chairman

2 points: 1) Executive of State Antislavery Society
2) State Convention Delegate
3) County Convention Chairman

1 point: 1) Executive Committee of County Antislavery Society
2) County Convention Delegate

3) Party District Leader
4) Any mention, report of speech, letter, etc., in anti-slavery newspapers

Having identified the four hundred most prominent abolitionists in New York from state antislavery sources, I then read leading nonantislavery sources—the *Albany Argus* and the *New York Tribune*—for the years 1840–1844 and assigned a point to a man each time he was mentioned in either publication. This procedure enabled me to rerank the names and to identify the two hundred most prominent abolitionists in the state. With these names at hand, I then began the third stage of my ranking procedure by reading a primary national antislavery source, the *Liberator*, for the years 1840–1844. A mention in this important journal was worth two points. After reranking the names according to points a second time, I selected the hundred most prominent abolitionist leaders in the state.[71] The three different procedures I followed yielded more or less the same results. The hundred most prominent abolitionists were generally the same on all three rankings. Several names were eliminated after some preliminary checkwork which yielded no information, and new names were added.

With these names I went to state histories, county histories, genealogies, local religious histories, and a variety of manuscript collections, including the monumental Gerrit Smith Collection at Syracuse University, to glean biographical information on the abolitionist leaders. In some cases, the amount and significance of information available acted as a criterion in rank determination, and therefore a slight shifting in the position of some of the abolitionists. However, at this stage the top one hundred remained the same, as did the top five.

[71] See Appendix 1.

In the following chapters I will attempt to explain who the abolitionist leaders were and what factors made it likely that they would tend to hold and take risks for the idea of abolitionism. I will also attempt to expose the process through which abolitionists came to total commitment.

2

The Five Top
Abolitionist Leaders
in New York State

BY the previously described method of rank determination, the five top abolitionist leaders in New York from 1838–1845 were Gerrit Smith, James G. Birney, Alvan Stewart, Beriah Green, and William Goodell.[1] Their respective biographical sketches which follow will give some indication as to who these abolitionists were, and in what ways they support or fail to support the tension-reduction interpretation of abolitionist leadership. In chapter 3, biographical sketches will be drawn of several other high-ranking abolitionist leaders in the

[1] Each of the top five abolitionist leaders scored at least 137 points. The range of scores for the next ten high ranking leaders discussed in chapter 3 was 112 to 50 points. The sixteenth highest score among the top 100 for whom biographical information could be found was only 43. Seven men with over 50 points (but not more than 68) are not described as among the top 15 due to a relative lack of biographical information. They are, however, included in the collective biography of the top 100 leaders.

state of New York; and in chapter 4, a composite portrait of abolitionist leadership, based on social variables, will be presented incorporating biographical information concerning the one hundred top New York abolitionist leaders.

The biographical sketches are important because abstract personality constructs are now coming under attack by psychologists as too far removed from the reality of individual people. It is argued that most psychological constructs account for the individual only as an "inert object wafted about in a public domain by external forces."[2]

It is important to note that the sketches which follow will be just that. Most of the men involved here and in chapter 3 have left voluminous collections of letters and manuscripts distributed throughout the United States, and many of them deserve book-length biographical treatment (three have received it), something obviously impossible within the scope of this work. The sketches will not be an attempt at definitiveness even in regard to the men's respective relationships to the antislavery movement, but will attempt to focus on each man's original motivation for joining the movement as far as this can be determined by an historian investigating written materials concerning men dead some hundred years.

Gerrit Smith

On 29 December 1874 the *New York Times* printed the following as part of an editorial obituary:

> The history of the most important half century of our national life will be imperfectly written if it fails to place Gerrit Smith in the front rank of men whose influence was most felt. . . .[3]

[2] George A. Kelly, *A Theory of Personality: The Psychology of Personal Constructs* (New York: W. W. Norton and Company, 1963), pp. 39–40.

[3] *New York Times*, 29 December 1874.

Yet Gerrit Smith, president of the New York Anti-Slavery Society 1836–1839 and one of the founders of the Liberty party, is generally ignored—even by professional historians, other than those specializing in antebellum America. The most recent biography of Smith was published almost thirty years ago and was, moreover, exceedingly hostile.[4]

Who was this man the *New York Times* thought was so significant?

Gerrit Smith was born in Utica, New York, 6 March 1797. He came to Peterboro, New York, at the age of nine, where he resided the greater part of his adult life. Smith's mother was Elizabeth Livingston, daughter of the notable James Livingston, and his father was Peter Smith whose ancestors were from Holland.[5]

Peter Smith's marriage into the Livingston family with its aristocratic connections among the Schuylers and the Van Rensselaers gave him considerable prestige. Peter, furthermore, had gained decided prestige on his own. In partnership with John Jacob Astor in the fur trade and other enterprises, and alone in real estate, Peter Smith managed to amass a considerable fortune. He turned over a $400,000 business to his son, Gerrit, in 1819 and bequeathed $800,000 more to his children in 1837. Smith was the county judge of Madison and has been described as "easily its leading citizen."[6]

Yet Peter Smith had the reputation of being "queer." Peter Skenandoah, one of Gerrit's brothers, was in middle life an alco-

---

[4] Ralph Harlow, *Gerrit Smith: Philanthropist and Reformer* (New York: Henry Holt and Company, 1939). Harlow, in an attempt to fit Smith into a preconceived profile of the abolitionists, tends to ignore a good deal of evidence he himself has marshaled.

[5] Ralph Harlow, "Gerrit Smith," *Dictionary of American Biography*, ed., by Allen Johnson, vol. 17 (New York: Charles Scribner's Sons, 1935), p. 270.

[6] Charles Hammond, *Gerrit Smith: The Story of a Noble Life* (Geneva, N.Y.: W. F. Humphrey, 1908), p. 6.

holic, in later life declared insane, and the younger brother, Adolphus Lent, has been described as "insane throughout his whole life."[7]

Despite this unfavorable aspect of Gerrit Smith's heritage, he came through his seventy-seven years with only one nervous breakdown, and that was of very short duration.

Gerrit attended Clinton Academy in Oneida County and was graduated with honors from Hamilton College in 1818. He was a fine scholar and delivered the valedictory address. He described his stay at the college as "very active with many friends."

On 11 January 1819 Smith married Wealtha Ann Backus, the daughter of the first president of Hamilton College; she died seven months later. Gerrit could not remain grief-stricken long, however, as his father's vast business interests and their concomitant responsibilities had been turned over to him. He now held land in all but six of the counties of New York State, as well as in Virginia, Vermont, and Michigan.[8]

Between 1819 and 1837 Smith became one of the most successful financiers in the state, investing much money in land and selling lots in farm-sized parcels. His management of his land was thus different from that of the great Hudson River proprietors who held their land in fee, assuring its ultimate reservation to the estate. Therefore Smith entirely escaped the antirent battles which for several years between 1839 and 1846 raged in the Hudson River region.

Like many others, Gerrit Smith was hurt by the depression of 1837. However, he borrowed a quarter of a million dollars from John Jacob Astor, retrenched, and by the mid-1840s was well on his way to rebuilding a monumental fortune. "For twenty-five years his income from Oswego averaged $50,000

[7] Harlow, *Gerrit Smith: Philanthropist and Reformer,* p. 3.

[8] E. P. Tanner, "Gerrit Smith: An Interpretation," *New-York Historical Association Quarterly* 5 (1924): 22–39.

or $60,000 a year, and during the last ten years of his life it equalled $80,000 annually."[9]

On 3 January 1822 Gerrit Smith married Ann Carole Fitzhugh of Livingston County, a relative of the Lees and Fitzhughs of Virginia. In 1826 Gerrit and his wife of four years joined the Presbyterian church. Ann had been hoping to convert Gerrit for some months, and on his birthday, 6 March 1826, she wrote to him: "I wish you many happy returns of this day, my dear husband, but with how much more joy would I celebrate it if it were the anniversary of your spiritual birth."[10]

A number of things made Ann's task relatively easy. Peter Smith was a devout and emotionally religious man, "constantly lamenting his sinfulness and seeking mercy;" and while Gerrit and his father had never been very close, they did become good friends following the death of Gerrit's mother. From 1822 on, Peter Smith was intensely engaged in the work of the Bible and Tract societies, both of which were evangelistic in aim.[11]

Furthermore, between 1825 and 1835 a series of religious revivals occurred in and around the area of Peterboro in central New York. The faithful in the community made persistent efforts to maintain religious fervor at a high pitch of intensity. "This long-continued and high-powered evangelistic

[9] Hammond, *Gerrit Smith*, p. 19. Smith, never enthusiastic about business, hired a representative to manage much of his enterprise—John B. Edwards (born 1802) of Oswego, New York. Edwards was one of New York's top one hundred abolitionist leaders and he worked for Smith for forty-three years. He was an excellent manager and a shrewd judge of real estate. Edwards was president of the Oswego County Savings Bank, president of the village, coroner, and trustee of the Oswego Library and Orphan Asylum (John C. Churchill, *Landmarks of Oswego County* [Syracuse: D. Mason, 1895], p. 313).

[10] Ann Smith to Gerrit Smith, 6 March 1826, Gerrit Smith Miller Collection, Syracuse University Manuscript Division, Syracuse, N.Y., GSMC.

[11] Harlow, *Gerrit Smith: Philanthropist and Reformer*, p. 51.

pressure," applied by the community, by Gerrit's beloved wife
and by his father, was probably responsible for Smith's
spiritual birth, and for his "entrance upon the work of re-
generating his fellow men."[12]

Gerrit Smith attended numerous revival meetings in the
early 1830s in search of "true faith" and the awakening of his
own benevolent impulses. "Pray for me, my dear wife," he
wrote to Ann, "that I may believe, that I may have true faith,
that my heart may be made clean. . . . Pray too that I may be
useful, and that this selfishness . . . give place to . . . benevolence."[13]

Smith's first systematic efforts at being useful were intimately connected with religion and began in the Sunday
school movement, moving off into the American Bible Society,
the Tract Society, and the American Home Missionary Society. One of the more curious missionary enterprises of this
period was the plan, originating in the mind of Gerrit Smith's
friend, J. T. Marshall, for converting France to evangelicalism
by means of sending Bibles and tracts to that country.

Gerrit Smith himself was less interested in evangelizing
France than in other reform projects nearer home. Blacks in
the southern states, for instance, needed more help than the
relatively fortunate Europeans. In October 1826, seven months
following his conversion, Smith was considering initiating a
seminary where Negro students might study for the ministry.[14]
In 1830 he began to think about a manual labor school for
blacks at Peterboro and in 1834 when his business ventures
became more promising, the school was opened.[15]

Ralph Randolph Gurley, secretary of the American Colonization Society, had begun in 1824 to advise Smith to spend his

12 Ibid.
13 Gerrit Smith to Ann Smith, 2 July 1832 [italics added], GSMC.
14 Professor Chester Dewey to Smith, 9 November 1826, GSMC.
15 *Liberator,* 8 November 1834.

money for schools in Liberia, the society's African colony. Smith did respond with a contribution;[16] and between 1828 and 1835 he donated at least $9,000.[17] By 1831, however, at the height of evangelistic fervor in New York State, Gerrit Smith wrote that the removal of free blacks from this country "without an eye to the great mass of slaves, is too limited and partial an object to awaken much feeling and exertion either at the North or the South."[18] But the colonization society had no intention of abolishing slavery, as Smith finally realized in 1835.

Even while he began to consider associating himself with the American Anti-Slavery Society which had been established in 1833, Smith retained his membership in the Colonization Society. He thought that the American Anti-Slavery Society should be less severe in its condemnation of "our young Christian brothers at the South, in whose inheritance are his deceased father's family servants, to whom he is aiming to do good on gospel principles, albeit he has not yet learned that these principles require him to dissolve the new relation he bears toward them."[19]

Smith remained a member of the Colonization Society for the greater part of 1835, and still believed early in that year that the main efforts of the antislavery societies should be in the direction of improving the condition of northern free Negroes in order to raise their status in the eyes of southern slaveholders.[20]

[16] Gurley to Smith, 21 November 1827 and 5 January 1828, GSMC.
[17] Harlow, *Gerrit Smith: Philanthropist and Reformer*, p. 63. He cites the following letters: Smith to Gurley, 16 October 1830; Smith to Walter Lourie, 31 December 1834; Smith to Gurley, 24 November 1835; Colonization Society Papers, Library of Congress.
[18] Smith to Gurley, 8 February 1831 and 8 November 1831, Colonization Society Papers.
[19] Smith to *Liberator,* 20 December 1834.
[20] Smith to *Friend of Man,* 2 February 1835.

In September 1835, Beriah Green[21] and Alvan Stewart[22] urged Smith to attend a convention at Utica for the purpose of organizing a state antislavery society. "Now is the time for men who have souls," wrote Green, "*to speak out.* . . . May God enable you in this matter to walk with him!"[23] On his arrival at Utica, Smith found the conservatives of the city determined to break up the convention by mob attack. As soon as the delegates assembled, the mob, led by a number of principal citizens including Congressman Samuel Beardsley, rushed in, reviled the abolitionists and compelled the convention to adjourn.

In November, Gerrit Smith asked to be enrolled in the New York State Anti-Slavery Society because the "Society is now so far identified with the right of free discussion . . . that if the Society be suffered to fall, the right of free discussion will fall with it."[24]

While this and similarly expressed sentiments might seem to qualify Smith as a fellow traveler, more interested in civil liberties than in slavery and free blacks, it is far more likely that the violence and suffering inflicted upon the abolitionists at Utica aroused in Smith such intense feelings as to make the ideas of the abolitionist victims more influential upon him.[25] It would be well to remember, too, that Smith had been

21 See p. 52.

22 See p. 57.

23 Green to Smith, 24 September 1835, GSMC.

24 Smith to Abraham Cox, 12 November 1835, quoted in Thomas Harwood, "British Evangelical Abolitionism and American Churches in the 1830's," *Journal of Southern History* 28 (August 1962): 303.

Abraham Cox (1800–1864) was one of New York State's one hundred top abolitionist leaders and a prominent American Presbyterian clergyman who had been converted at a church conference in Scotland in summer 1833 from support of colonization to abolitionism.

25 See Silvan Tomkins, "The Psychology of Commitment: The Constructive Role of Violence and Suffering for the Individual and his Society," in *Antislavery Vanguard*, ed. by Martin Duberman (Princeton: Princeton University Press, 1964), pp. 295–296.

deeply concerned over slavery and the condition of free Negroes for almost ten years prior to the Utica affair.

Yet even as a member of this abolitionist group Smith's first
suggestions about emancipation were hesitant and relatively
mild. As late as April 1838, Gerrit Smith believed that the
primary job of the Anti-Slavery Society was simply to "publish
the truth about slavery," and nothing more.[26] In the face of
suggestions to establish an independent *political* organization
for abolitionists, Smith expressed fears that the organization
of a separate party would "endanger the purity of our principles and diminish our just reliance on the efficacy of moral
truth."[27]

It soon became obvious, however, that moral suasion was
not bringing the desired results. In addition, antiabolitionist
propaganda and action were intensifying. Still, at the 1838
convention of the American Anti-Slavery Society Smith continued to express the belief that southern slaveholders could
be converted to antislavery principles, but he indicated that
he agreed at least in part with Alvan Stewart's notion that
abolitionists should move the slavery question into the political arena.

And during the political campaign of 1838, in an attempt
to initiate a balance of power strategy by abolitionists, Smith
agreed to put a series of questions[28] to some of the political

---

[26] Smith to *Friend of Man*, 4 April 1838.

[27] Smith to *Friend of Man*, 11 July 1838.

[28] The questions put to the candidates were: "Are you in favor of
granting trial by jury to persons in New York claimed as fugitive slaves?
Do you favor the removal of all distinctions which are 'founded solely on
complexion' in the constitutional rights of citizens of New York? Do you
favor repeal of the law which now makes it possible for persons to bring
slaves into New York and hold them there for not more than nine
months?" (*Emancipator*, 30 October 1838).

Political activity was not foreign to Smith: he wrote an address to the
voters of Madison County in winter 1823 which was a plea for the extension of the popular election of officials, was nominated for state Senate

leaders in New York including William Seward and Governor Marcy in order to determine which candidates abolitionists should support at the polls. The 1838 election results demonstrated that so long as only a relatively small number of men in New York cared intensely enough about "abolishing slavery to be willing to desert their parties, no benefit would accrue to the major party which identified itself with that position. Gains acquired by propitiating abolitionists would be counterbalanced by losses suffered from antagonizing antiabolitionists."[29] This frustration, on top of increasing southern intransigence and northern antiabolitionist antagonism, pushed the abolitionists and Gerrit Smith further along the path to final commitment.

At the Central New York Anti-Slavery Convention in 1839, Gerrit Smith called for abolitionists to help fugitive slaves escape—marking the first time that an antislavery leader asked for any illegal activity to further the cause.[30] And between 1839 and February 1840 Gerrit Smith changed from opposition to support of a northern movement to organize an independent abolitionist party and present a presidential ticket in 1840.[31]

After becoming an abolitionist, Smith was placed in the uncomfortable position of giving indirect sanction to the sin of slavery by remaining in the Presbyterian church.[32] He sub-

---

on the Anti-Masonic ticket in 1827 and 1831, and attended a Whig State Convention in 1834 (A. J. Northrup, "Gerrit Smith," n.d., n.p., at Madison County Historical Society, Oneida, N.Y.).

[29] Lee Benson, *Concept of Jacksonian Democracy* (Princeton: Princeton University Press, 1961), p. 112.

[30] *Friend of Man*, 2 July 1839.

[31] The success of the independent party ticket would secure the political balance of power that most New York abolitionists wanted and would help their organization attract abolitionists still tied to William Lloyd Garrison, who opposed any political action and insisted that the work of moral suasion go on much as it had before 1837.

[32] While many abolitionist leaders were Presbyterians, not many Presbyterians were abolitionists. The official position of the church came close

jected the Peterboro minister to sharp attack and wrote, "I regard a presbyterian church or methodist church as no church."[33] But finally Smith withdrew from the church in December 1843, at the same time helping to create a local nondenominational abolitionist church. He went on to further religious reform for the next thirty years,[34] ultimately refusing to accept the Bible as the final and infallible guide to religious truth. An abolitionist colleague wrote to him, "I must keep out of your way, unless I am prepared to allow myself to be seduced, by your precepts and example from the orthodox standards—into true reform, nay into christianity with a Christ in it!"[35]

Religious reform and social reform were inseparable for Smith as for most other abolitionists. And thus while the church and society remained immovable, in fact became more defensive and antagonistic about the "evils" housed in each, Smith and the abolitionists grew more militant.

Smith's speeches, letters, and printed pamphlets took on a more and more denunciatory, contentious tone.

By 1847 Gerrit Smith was convinced that the prospect of the two major parties showing any intelligent sense of their obligations was so remote that the Liberty party could do nothing but aspire to a permanent place in American politics.[36]

---

to the sentiment of Reverend E. P. Barrows of the First Free Presbyterian Church of New York who believed that it would be unfair to condemn slaveholders to the point of barring them from church membership, because the conditions under which emancipation might be accomplished were so difficult (*A View of the American Slavery Question* [New York: J. S. Taylor, 1836], passim; Lorman Ratner, "Northern Opposition to the Antislavery Crusade 1830–1840" [Ph.D. diss., Cornell University, 1960], pp. 134 ff).

33 Gerrit Smith to William Goodell, 22 January 1842, GSMC. For Goodell, see p. 57.

34 Ralph V. Harlow, "Gerrit Smith and the Free Church Movement," *New York History* 18 (July 1937): 277.

35 George Washington Jonson to Gerrit Smith, 13 December 1847, GSMC. Jonson, one of the one hundred top abolitionist leaders, was a graduate of Dartmouth College and a lawyer.

36 Gerrit Smith to *Emancipator*, 23 August 1847.

And after the passage of a strengthened Fugitive Slave Act in 1850, the repeal of the Missouri Compromise in 1854 (an antislavery measure on the statute books for over thirty years), the misuse of the federal government by the Pierce and Buchanan administrations to make Kansas sure for slavery, and the Dred Scott decision making slavery legal in all territories of the United States, Smith could write, "We must not shrink from fighting for Liberty and if Federal troops fight against her, we must fight against them."[37]

By 1859 Smith was ready to give moral and financial support to John Brown and become an accessory before the fact in the raid at Harper's Ferry.[38] After the raid he was haunted with the idea that he was responsible for the lives that were lost on account of Brown's project. Five days after Brown was sentenced to death on 2 November 1859 Gerrit Smith suffered a nervous collapse and was taken to the New York State Asylum for the Insane at Utica.

The contemporary medical opinion was that the "Harper's Ferry shock only hastened the development of a disease which at no very remote period would have appeared in a more unfavorable form."[39] Given Smith's amazingly speedy recovery, however, it is more likely that he was suffering from an extreme case of guilty conscience.

As we have seen, Gerrit Smith did not become "unshakably convinced of the righteousness of [his] cause" overnight.[40] The pathway from early resonance induced by his father, his wife, and an evangelistic context, to final commitment was not without internal conflict.[41] At various times Gerrit Smith

[37] Gerrit Smith to Thaddeus Hyatt, 25 July 1857, Kansas State Historical Society, Topeka, Kan.

[38] Harlow, *Gerrit Smith: Philanthropist and Reformer*, p. 409.

[39] Dr. Gray (head of asylum) to John Cochrane (Smith's nephew), 16 December 1859, GSMC.

[40] Rudolf Heberle, *Psychology of Social Movements* (New York: Appleton-Century-Crofts, 1951), p. 116.

[41] See chapter 1.

suffered doubt whether to give himself completely to abolitionism. The decision was made after considerable reflection. The stages in the development of Smith's commitment to abolitionism were certainly not brought on by any economic or social dislocation. One of the richest men in New York State, Gerrit Smith possessed the enormous power which money brings, as well as a high social position.[42]

There are strong hints that psychological infirmities were a family trait: the "insanity" of two brothers, the "queerness" of the father—Gerrit himself spent seven weeks in an asylum. Without denying the possibility that this has some significance, we can legitimately ask how to demonstrate it when the first real evidence of Gerrit's "infirmity" appeared in 1859, thirty-three years after he interested himself in black Americans and some twenty years after he committed himself to abolitionism.

There is also definite evidence of irascibility, bitterness, and even vindictiveness. But, to speak exclusively of Smith's abusive qualities is to ignore the considerable evidence of personal warmth and kindness. "In his relations with his assistants and agents, with one exception, Smith was uniformly considerate and kindly . . . . In his home Gerrit Smith showed deep affection for his wife . . . . As a father [he] resembled the general run of well-disposed but very busy men."[43]

After Appomattox, while Smith continued to insist strenuously that blacks were entitled to full social as well as political equality, endorsing the view that landed estates be subdivided and parceled out,[44] he was one of the signers of the bail bond

[42] E. P. Tanner, "Gerrit Smith," p. 26.

[43] Harlow, *Gerrit Smith: Philanthropist and Reformer*, p. 41.

[44] Gerrit Smith distributed approximately 140,000 acres of his own land in northern New York to 3,000 Negroes in 1848 and 1849. However, the cost of moving, settling, seeding, and waiting for the first crops compelled many Negroes to abandon their grants. The failure was not so much in the idea, as in implementation without "total planning" (*North Star*, 7 January, 18 February, 1848; 5 January, 2 March, 1 June, 1849).

to release Jefferson Davis from captivity and advocated a policy of moderation and mercy toward the South.

That Gerrit Smith's original resonance to antislavery was a function of the influence exerted upon him by his father's and his wife's and his community's religious convictions appears credible. It is undeniable that frustration turned his antislavery into the more radical abolitionism. The frustration, however, does not seem to have been a result of social or economic dislocation or psychic conflict, but the result of punishment and suffering in the form of verbal abuse, actual violence against Smith and his colleagues, the increasing antagonism of opponents, and most important, the inability to achieve a literal attainment of the desired results.

James G. Birney

James Gillespie Birney, presidential candidate of the abolitionist Liberty party in 1840 and again in 1844, was born in Kentucky, 4 February 1792. He "had every advantage of birth and circumstance, his home being that of the typical aristocratic family" of the Bluegrass State.[45]

His father, James Birney, an Irish expatriate, emigrated to America in 1783, and in 1788 moved to Kentucky, where he became one of the wealthiest men in the state.[46]

James Gillespie Birney had been left motherless at the age of three, and his relationship with his father developed into one of great affection. The elder Birney believed not only in

---

[45] Betty Fladeland, *James Gillespie Birney: Slaveholder to Abolitionist* (Ithaca: Cornell University Press, 1955), p. 1.

[46] William MacDonald, "James Gillespie Birney," *Dictionary of American Biography*, ed. by Allen Johnson, vol. 2 (New York: Charles Scribner's Sons, 1929), p. 291.

Christian good works, but more specifically had, along with *his* father, fought to make Kentucky a free state. He "held that emancipation by the state legislature on an over-all basis was the only solution to the problem and that until that day came one had to be kind to slaves and to protect them."[47] Furthermore, Aunt Doyle, the older Birney's sister, who came from Ireland to take charge of the Birney household after the death of Mrs. Birney, refused to own a slave and would not accept the services of her brother's slaves without paying them. Mrs. Doyle, who "soon became as dear as a mother to young James" and his sister Nancy, constantly spoke of "the stirring antislavery sermons" she had heard "Father" David Rice, a Presbyterian minister, preach in Kentucky in the 1790s.[48]

Birney's exposure to his father's and grandfather's political and religious activity and his aunt's religious sentiments provided a model which predisposed the future abolitionist to be attracted to movements based on public service, and particularly antislavery. This model was reinforced at Transylvania University where Birney's mentor, Robert Hamilton Bishop, made an outstanding reputation as an opponent of slavery, and where the president of the college, Reverend Samuel Stanhope Smith, had written a book which held that differences between black men and white men would be obliterated as the Negro was exposed to American civilization.[49]

After graduating from Princeton University in 1810, James G. Birney read law in the office of Alexander J. Dallas in Philadelphia.[50] Dallas was a man imbued with the idea of public service, and conversations with him reiterated many of the things Birney had heard at home about slavery. The

47 Fladeland, *James Gillespie Birney*, p. 7.
48 Ibid.
49 Samuel Stanhope Smith, *An Essay on the Causes of the Variety of Complexion and Figure in the Human Species* (New Brunswick, New Jersey, 1810).
50 MacDonald, "James Gillespie Birney," p. 291.

original resonance induced at the Kentucky plantation of James's boyhood was constantly reinforced in his young manhood. He was admitted to the bar in 1814, and began an important practice at Danville. On 1 February 1816 he married Agatha McDowell, daughter of United States District Judge William McDowell and niece of Governor George McDowell of Kentucky.[51] This marriage brought him some slaves.

In early 1816 he was elected to the town council, and in August to the state legislature. Yet he removed two years later to Madison County, Alabama for "better opportunity." Here the Birneys quickly moved into the fast-moving gay life of the southern planting aristocracy.[52] James was elected in 1819 to the state legislature of Alabama, "but his opposition to a resolution endorsing the candidacy of Andrew Jackson for president was unpopular, and he was not reelected."[53]

Birney had already attained marked prominence as a lawyer, but because of his cotton crop failure in 1821 and too frequent gambling, he was forced to sell his plantation and remove to Huntsville.[54] "At Huntsville his legal practice shortly recouped his finances, and thereafter, for most of his life, he was comparatively wealthy."[55] The Birneys became established as "one of Huntsville's leading families." James and Agatha were active in community affairs, she in the Presbyterian church, he in government and education.[56]

In 1826, mainly through the influence of his wife, James Birney became a Presbyterian. Birney's conversion was something more than a formal joining of the church: "Old things passed away; . . . all things were become new."[57] Henceforth,

51 Ibid.
52 Fladeland, *James G. Birney*, p. 19.
53 MacDonald, "James Gillespie Birney," p. 291.
54 Fladeland, *James Gillespie Birney*, p. 21.
55 MacDonald, "James Gillespie Birney," pp. 291–292.
56 Fladeland, *James G. Birney*, p. 28.
57 Quoted in ibid., p. 31.

he believed, his life should be measured by more than the worldly recompense of a successful career and prosperity. Birney hoped that his relatives, friends, and law associates would also find the "vision of the better life."[58]

At the time of his conversion Birney consented, after having refused in 1824, to be legal counsel to the Cherokee Indians who were being forced off their lands in Georgia. It was at this time also that his interest in the domestic slave trade and the colonization movement was strongly aroused.[59]

He drafted a bill to give effect to the provision of the Alabama constitution prohibiting the importation of slaves for sale. This bill was passed after much struggle in January 1827, but to Birney's chagrin was repealed in 1829 following the election of Jackson.[60] The opposition Birney had encountered in getting his bill passed deepened his early commitment but it also raised, at least temporarily, serious doubts about the wisdom of such a commitment. Birney wrote in 1828, "It [is] hard to tell what one's duty [is] toward the poor creatures; but I have made up my mind to one thing . . . . I will not allow them to be treated brutally."[61]

James G. Birney's hope of converting southerners to antislavery was frustrated even further as he watched with dismay the violent and repressive reaction of whites to the Nat Turner rebellion in summer, 1831. White response included tightening restraints on free blacks as well as slaves and an increased antagonism to abolitionists. Birney took this opportunity to reintroduce his bill of 1827 against importation of slaves which passed once more in January 1832 but with several

---

58 Ibid., p. 31.
59 MacDonald, "James Gillespie Birney," p. 292.
60 Ibid. While Birney had strongly disapproved of the policy of attacking Jackson personally, he had accepted nomination as a presidential elector on the Adams ticket in 1828.
61 Quoted in William Birney, *James G. Birney and His Times* (New York: D. Appleton & Co., 1890), p. 12.

reactionary amendments that, among other things, prohibited the teaching of any black person to read or write and provided the death penalty for anyone circulating "seditious or incendiary literature."[62]

The one part of the bill Birney supported, the prohibition of the slave trade, was repealed in December 1832, increasing his frustration. This reactionary trend made Birney rather desperate over the South's future and increased his determination to leave.[63]

In summer 1832 Birney, still struggling to find a right course for his life, had a series of conversations with the important abolitionist Theodore Dwight Weld. No doubt Weld's conviction and enthusiasm were factors influencing Birney's decision to accept the agency of the American Colonization Society.[64] But Birney did not make up his mind quickly. The pathway from early resonance to final commitment, for Birney as for Gerrit Smith, was not without internal conflict. Birney wrote to the secretary of the Colonization Society of his dilemma: "The call given by your Society—to all appearance, providential—added to the earnest resistance of many of my most esteemed religious friends to my project of removing from amongst them, has really staggered me not a little."[65] And during that summer, Birney, in order to have time to study the subject of colonization, rejected all new professional business. In August he finally accepted a commission as agent of the American Colonization Society, and for some months traveled and lectured in the South.[66]

As he toured the South and saw more of the institution of slavery, and as he spoke more on the subject, he became more

[62] Birney, *James G. Birney and His Times*, p. 104.
[63] Fladeland, *James G. Birney*, p. 49.
[64] Ibid., p. 53.
[65] Birney to Gurley, 12 July 1832, American Colonization Society Papers.
[66] MacDonald, "James Gillespie Birney," p. 292.

and more convinced that the slave system was not only dangerous but sinful. He wrote at the beginning of 1833:

> My mind is ill at ease upon the subject of retaining my fellow creatures in servitude. I cannot, nor do I believe any honest mind can, reconcile the precept "love thy neighbor as thyself" with the purchase of the body of that neighbor and consigning him to a slavery, a perpetual bondage degrading and debasing him in this world and almost excluding him from the happiness of that which is to come.[67]

In April 1834 Birney visited Oberlin College where Theodore Dwight Weld and other students took him in hand and "expounded unto him the way of God more perfectly." In May, "convinced that colonization would increase the interstate slave trade, and unable to reconcile it with his views of religion and justice, Birney resigned"[68] his offices in both the Colonization Society and the Kentucky Society for the Gradual Relief of the State from Slavery. In June he freed his slaves and allied himself with the more aggressive antislavery forces. And by July, after James G. Birney discovered that wherever he went "in Danville or in neighboring towns, he had come to expect to be lectured by old friends, to be 'roundly abused' by others,"[69] he wrote to Weld:

> I have not one helper—not one from whom I can draw sympathy, or impart joy, on this topic! . . . my nearest friends . . . think it very silly in me to run against the world in a matter that cannot in any way do me any good . . . . Even my own children . . . look upon my views as chimerical and visionary . . . my nearest friends here are of the sort that are always crying out "take care of

---

[67] Birney to Gurley, 24 January 1833, American Colonization Society Papers.
[68] MacDonald, "James Gillespie Birney," p. 292.
[69] Fladeland, *James G. Birney*, p. 90.

yourself—don't meddle with other people's affairs—do nothing, say nothing, get along quietly—make money. . . ."

To this end I see very plainly my private affairs are hastening. I do not believe I can remain in Kentucky.[70]

From this sense of loneliness and depression, induced not only by Birney's inability to convert southerners to antislavery, but southerners' increasing antagonism toward him, he could get no relief from his church. Disputes between the "new" and "old" school[71] seemed to be dominating everyone's attention to the exclusion of slavery. "Christian action will still be hindered in angry dispute," wrote Birney in his diary. "Oh, Lord! let it not be so . . . .[72]

By March 1835, Birney was active in forming the Kentucky Anti-Slavery Society, and in May, at the New York meeting of the American Anti-Slavery Society, he strongly urged united action by all opponents of slavery.[73] A visit to New England, after the New York meeting, was interrupted by news of outspoken hostility to the publication of Birney's antislavery weekly, the first issue of which was planned for August 1. He escaped an angry mob on his return, but the publication of the paper was delayed.[74]

This and similar happenings led Birney, even after he had

[70] Birney to Weld, 17 July 1834, Birney Collection, Library of Congress.

[71] "New School" divinity was based upon "the sufficiency of human reason in matters of religion," as against the orthodox view which emphasized faith and ministerial interpretation. "The New School contained Northern moderates, as well as Southern members, who were opposed to antislavery agitation, but those synods which had declared against the 'sin' of slaveholding had strong New School leanings" (Bruce C. Steiger, "Abolitionism and the Presbyterian Schism of 1837–1838," *Mississippi Valley Historical Review*, 36 [December 1949]: 391–414).

[72] Diary, 30 September 1834, quoted in Fladeland, *James G. Birney*, p. 98.

[73] American Anti-Slavery Society, *Second Annual Report of the American Anti-Slavery Society* (New York: William S. Dorr, 1836), passim.

[74] MacDonald, "James Gillespie Birney," p. 292.

apparently firmly committed himself to abolitionism, to write to Gerrit Smith:

> I am at times greatly perplexed. To have alienated from us those with whom we [went] up from Sabbath to Sabbath to the house of God—many of our connections and relations estranged from us, and the whole Community with but here and there an exception, looking upon you as an enemy to its peace is no small trial.[75]

He might bear such opposition and criticism for himself, but his father, his wife, and his children would also be targets. Already his sons had been taunted and jeered by playmates.[76] The continuance of opposition helped him make up his mind to move to Ohio.

In 1836 after a convention of the Ohio Anti-Slavery Society at Granville, Birney was egged; at Xenia, he was egged again; at Columbus, the mob followed him to his lodgings, and the next day he found it impossible to obtain a place to speak again.[77] Thus Birney discovered he was to meet violence in response to his pro-Negro activity in the North as well as in the South, and on several more occasions "he was exposed to personal danger; meetings at which he spoke were interrupted, and his paper suffered." And the office of his printer was completely destroyed.[78]

In spring 1837, Birney's suffering and frustration were increased further by an indictment against him in Cincinnati for harboring in his home an escaped slave, Matilda, who had

[75] Birney to Smith, 14 July 1835, Birney Collection, Library of Congress.
[76] Fladeland, *James G. Birney*, p. 122.
[77] Described in letters from Birney to Tappan, 29 April 1836 and 2 May 1836, Tappan Collection, Library of Congress. For Tappan, see p. 71.
[78] Birney wrote that the action of the mob had won people to the cause by the thousands, when only tens had been added before, indicating once more the credibility of Silvan Tomkins's view that violence inflicted on the abolitionists led others to take up their cause.

been claimed and returned as a fugitive, and more significantly by James Birney, Sr.'s, command that if his son did not at once give up the *Philanthropist,* his antislavery weekly, all intercourse between them must cease.[79]

It was after all this that Birney became one of the foremost representatives and outspoken leaders of those who sought to emancipate slaves by political action as well as by moral suasion.[80]

James G. Birney, eminently successful lawyer, considerably wealthy most of his life, and extremely popular as evidenced by frequent elections to important local and statewide offices, was not a victim of economic or social dislocation, at least not until his antislavery commitment.

Birney was first attracted to the problem of slavery not out of any need to reduce "tension" he was feeling, but out of direct sympathy for the slave induced by his own experience and by his family context of moral and Christian zeal combined with great affection. Yet even after his conversion, as an adult, to Presbyterian evangelicalism in 1826, he was attracted not to abolitionism, at first, but to the program of the American Colonization Society. And it was some time before he committed himself wholeheartedly even to this relatively mild organization.

It was to be several more years, after a process of continuing alternation between opposition, violence, suffering, and partial victory which stimulated rising expectations constantly frustrated, that Birney finally committed himself to abolitionism.

Birney held back because he was not quickly convinced that slaveholders could not be reached by reason: and he was more interested in improving his beloved South than in destroying the slaveholder. But Birney met violence in response to his pro-Negro activity. He was terribly disappointed at the in-

[79] Fladeland, *James G. Birney,* pp. 147–155.
[80] MacDonald, "James Gillespie Birney," p. 292.

transigence of the South, the turning away of former friends, the loss of status, and the increasing alienation between his father and himself.

Yet Birney's determination to confront both censure and threats of physical violence increased. Believing that men must "themselves die freemen [rather] than slaves, or our country, glorious as has been her hope, is gone forever,"[81] Birney gave up a lucrative law practice, influence, and respect in his community, and his inheritance to commit himself to the cause of freeing the slaves. And as he wrote, "When I remember how calmly and dispassionately my mind has proceeded from truth to truth connected with this subject [slavery] to another still higher I feel satisfied that my conclusions are not the fruits of enthusiasm."[82]

Alvan Stewart

Unlike Gerrit Smith and James G. Birney, Alvan Stewart, one of the first New York abolitionists to urge independent political action on behalf of the slave[83] and the future gubernatorial candidate of the Liberty party, was born to farm parents in only moderate circumstances. His career was an upward struggle from obscurity.

Born on 1 September 1790 in South Granville, Washington

81 *Philanthropist,* 23 September 1836.
82 James G. Birney, *Letter on Colonization* (New York: American Anti-Slavery Society, 1834), p. 45.
83 Myron Holley (1779–1841), graduate of Williams College, member of the New York State Assembly, 1816, was advocating separate antislavery nominations along with Stewart. Long involved in political reform including the Anti-Masonic movement, Holley wrote in 1839 "Abolitionists should . . . purify political life, at present the most potent source of social control" (Holley to Joshua Leavitt, 23 July 1839 in *Emancipator,* 15 August 1839).

County, New York, Alvan went with his family to Westford, Vermont, in 1795 where they sought "better opportunity." He eventually attended common school there, and in the winter of 1808, at the age of seventeen, began teaching school and at the same time studying anatomy and medicine.

With the money he continued to earn from teaching part-time, he paid his tuition at the University of Vermont at Burlington. At commencement he delivered the Greek oration. After graduation in 1813 he continued to teach school and began the study of law at Cherry Valley, New York. Stewart practiced law there for sixteen years.[84]

He "devoted himself to his profession with such pecuniary success that he acquired considerable property and gained the reputation of an eminent lawyer."[85] Stewart "was successful in the accumulation of property far beyond those whose business was greatly superior to his own."[86]

For many years he was fond of politics, but according to a contemporary observer "not a successful politician . . . he always managed to enlist in the weaker and unsuccessful side."[87] Despite this failure of judgment, Stewart managed to get himself elected mayor of Cherry Valley at the age of thirty-one.[88] He was a consistent advocate of protective duties, internal improvements, and public education, early aligning himself with the Whigs.

In 1830, at the height of the revival movement in central New York, Stewart wrote to his parents:

[84] This information was gleaned from handwritten notes by Luther R. Marsh in the Stewart Collection, New York State Historical Association, Cooperstown, N.Y.

[85] L. B. Proctor, *Bench and Bar of New York* (New York: Diossy and Company, 1870), p. 217.

[86] Levi Beardsley, *Reminiscences of Otsego* (New York: n.p., 1852), p. 169.

[87] Ibid.

[88] Alice Henderson, "History of the New York State Anti-Slavery Society" (Ph.D. diss., University of Michigan, 1963), p. 59.

I hope I continue to search after the everlasting Riches of Christ and never mean to cease speaking and performing what I consider that the Rules of Christianity impose on a humble suppliant at the foot of the Cross. . . . What I regret is that so many of my days have run to waste and have not been spent in serving that God before whom we must all shortly appear to render up an account of our stewardship here on earth.[89]

By 1832, Stewart was making slavery and temperance his life's work, and in 1835 he found that his antislavery activities did not permit him full-time legal practice.[90] He "embraced the cause of northern abolitionism, which he advocated to such an extent as greatly to impair his influence. . . . It was the end of his chance for political preferment."[91] Thus he moved into a "sphere where there were few applauding voices . . . ." In fact, "he accepted a position that brought upon him scorn and anathema."[92]

The October 1835 meeting at Utica to organize the New York State Anti-Slavery Society was disrupted by a mob and Stewart was physically as well as verbally attacked. Rumors indicated that a night attack was contemplated upon Mr. Stewart's house. And the next day as the convention proceeded to Peterboro, at the invitation of Gerrit Smith, to continue their deliberations, the abolitionists, Stewart among them, were pelted with stones, mud, and rotten eggs.[93] To add insult to injury, a suit was brought against some of the abolitionists for inciting the mob to riot.

This constant opposition from all quarters not only in-

[89] Alvan Stewart to Uriel Stewart, 12 July 1830, Stewart Manuscript, New-York Historical Society, New York, N.Y.

[90] Henderson, "History of the New York State Anti-Slavery Society," p. 60.

[91] Beardsley, *Reminiscences of Otsego*, p. 169.

[92] Proctor, *Bench and Bar*, p. 237.

[93] Luther R. Marsh, *Writings and Speeches of Alvan Stewart on Slavery* (New York: A. B. Burdick, 1860), p. 16.

creased the ranks of the abolitionists,[94] but increased Stewart's resonance to the movement, his identification with the oppressed Negro, and his hostility toward the oppressor. Between 1835 and 1839 he donated $1,200 and eighteen months of his time to the New York State Anti-Slavery Society.[95]

Opposition came from high places as well as from mobs. Stewart wrote in reference to the closing off of congressional discussion of slavery in 1836: "We should fear no gag laws; it is what we want if our enemies dare make them."[96] While recognizing that the violation of civil liberties added fellow travelers and even abolitionists to the lists, Stewart was happier when there was no opposition and "the days of the mobs [were] gone by. . . . We are gaining," he wrote, "our cause goes forward with great success."[97]

Stewart's confidence in the cause was deflated somewhat in 1838–1839 when he realized that he was at least one step ahead of his antislavery colleagues in his interpretation of congressional power vis-à-vis slavery, and when he saw that the questioning of major party candidates, the original political tactic of the abolitionists, failed to achieve a political balance of power for antislavery men.

Stewart now believed "If we ever strike a political blow for the slave we must go deep . . . ."[98] He contended, basing his

---

[94] Alvan Stewart wrote: "Permit me to assure you, that the attempt of the mob at Utica, to suppress free discussion by a convention of more than five hundred men, as respectable as any body of persons who ever met for the public good, on this continent, has been the direct means of adding thousands to the abolitionists." Quoted in Marsh, *Writings and Speeches*, p. 72.

[95] *Friend of Man*, 23 October 1839.

[96] Alvan Stewart to William Goodell, 26 March 1836, Goodell Papers, Berea College, Berea, Ky.).

[97] Stewart to Lewis Tappan, 11 February 1836, Tappan Collection, Library of Congress.

[98] Stewart to E. W. Clarke, 14 September 1839, Slavery Manuscripts, New-York Historical Society, New York. E. W. Clarke (1801–1886), one of

argument upon the due process clause of the constitution, that slaves were deprived of their freedom without due process of law, and that slavery itself was therefore a violation of the constitution. In a letter to his wife, Stewart described what happened at the 1838 meeting of the American Anti-Slavery Society when he attempted to persuade that group to this view: "I have argued my constitutional argument for two days. Mr. William Jay, Mr. Birney, Mr. Leavitt . . . and many others came down upon me like a thunder shower . . . . The vote was finally taken and there was 47 for me and 37 against me, 10 majority—*immense victory.*"[99] In fact, however, this was a defeat, as a two-thirds vote was necessary for success.

Stewart was the first not only to elaborate the argument that the federal government could legally destroy slavery in the states, but also to insist "earnestly in . . . consultations, in committees and elsewhere on the necessity of forming a distinct political party to promote the abolition of slavery."[100]

In 1842, ten years after Alvan Stewart had taken his first risk on behalf of the slave and initiated the process of opposition, violence, and suffering which induced his frustration, he wrote:

We have appealed to the Church, and she has declined the honor. We appealed to Congress and she threw us back our petitions, mixed with broken fragments of the Constitution. We have ap-

---

the top one hundred abolitionists in New York State, practiced law in Oswego County until 1846 when he went with the Northwestern Insurance Company. He was a participant in the balance of power strategy —"If you should get but 100 votes for your ticket, that small number would probably turn the question and satisfy one of the parties that you had beaten it, even without victory, you will have success" (Stewart to Clarke, 21 October 1839, Slavery Manuscripts).

99 Stewart to wife, 7 May 1838, Stewart Collection, New York State Historical Society.

100 William Goodell, quoted in Marsh, *Writings and Speeches,* p. 27.

pealed to the slaveholder! He points to the fagot and the flames
—We have tried the . . . system of questioning the political candidates in this land; hoping by that lever to pry open the prison
doors,—We never by this course, gained truth an advocate, or
humanity a friend.[101]

The frustration evident in this letter led Stewart to a position which distinguished him and other political abolitionists
from the moral suasion, nonresistance Garrisonians: "The
object of all law is, to save society from violence and in-
justice. Moral suasion is not sufficient to protect the weak from
the power of the strong . . . ."[102]

Like Smith and Birney, Stewart achieved a position of high
social status and accumulated a good deal of property. Very
much like Birney he gave up his status and a lucrative law
practice to devote his life to freeing slaves. The only significant
frustration he seems to have suffered occurred *after* his commitment to antislavery when his religious and legal precepts
were abused and "he was roughly used by the advocates of
the system he was opposing."[103]

Beriah Green

Born on 24 March 1795 in Preston, a small town in western
Connecticut, Beriah Green was the eldest son of farm parents
who were intense Congregationalists. Beriah was trained by
his family in a strict Calvinism.

In 1810 the Greens moved to Vermont. Five years later

[101] Stewart to Dr. Bailey, April 1842, quoted in Marsh, *Writings and
Speeches*, p. 263.

[102] Copy of Stewart notes by Luther Marsh in Stewart Collection,
New York Historical Association.

[103] Marsh, *Writings and Speeches*, p. 71.

Beriah entered Kimball Union Academy, a college prepara-
tory school in New Hampshire; and in 1816 he enrolled in
Middlebury College in Vermont. Three years later the Master
of Arts degree was conferred upon him.[104]

In 1820 in order to prepare himself for missionary work in
the service of the American Board of Commissioners for
Foreign Missions, Beriah Green entered Andover Theological
Seminary. While attending, he taught in Phillips Andover
Academy to defray his expenses. However, within a year his
health became too poor for missionary work, and he was
licensed as a minister by the New London Association.[105]

Green was formally ordained 16 April 1823 in Brandon,
Vermont. He served six years in the Congregational church
there, becoming comparatively well known in religious and
educational circles, frequently contributing to such periodicals
as *Christian Spectator, Vermont Chronicle, Home Missionary
and American Pastor's Journal,* and *Spirit of the Pilgrims.*[106]

In 1830 Green was unanimously chosen by the board of
trustees to hold a professorship of sacred literature at Western
Reserve College, where he also served as college chaplain. At
this relatively high point in his career, holding a prestigious
position, Beriah Green was exposed to Theodore Dwight Weld
who visited Western Reserve in autumn 1832. Less than two
months after Weld departed, Green was preaching abolitionism from the chapel pulpit.[107]

The trustees of Western Reserve College were opposed to
slavery but preferred the milder program of the American
Colonization Society. Green felt it was necessary for him to

104 Muriel L. Block, "Beriah Green the Reformer" (Master's thesis,
Syracuse University, 1935), pp. 1–2; W. Randall Waterman, "Beriah
Green," *Dictionary of American Biography,* ed. by Allen Johnson, vol.
7 (New York: Charles Scribner's Sons, 1931), p. 540.
105 Ibid.
106 Block, "Beriah Green the Reformer," p. 6.
107 Ibid., p. 13.

take a risk on behalf of the slave at this point "to expose the noxious tendencies, and counteract the deadly influence of such doctrines" as colonization.[108] As a consequence of taking this risk, Beriah suffered at the hands of several members of the board of trustees. The situation grew so uncomfortable for Green that he was forced to resign his position on 20 June 1833. He moved to Oneida Institute in the vicinity of Utica, becoming its president.[109]

By late 1835, even before the mob action at Utica, Beriah Green was again feeling uncomfortable due to the efforts of antiabolitionists. He wrote to Gerrit Smith:

> [Southerners] forbid us to say anything on the subject. . . . Men may say what they will of the value of the Union; but where is the Union when the mail is robbed in open day with impunity; and when . . . men dare not attend a missionary meeting . . . for fear of being murdered?[110]

His discomfort and frustration were further increased when state Senator Wager of Utica began an onslaught against Green and his institute. In March 1836, the senator had proposed a resolution which was adopted by the senate, "directing the Committee on Literature to inquire into the propriety of denying the Oneida Institute all participation in the benefits of the Literature Fund." It was alleged, in support of this resolution that the

> Oneida Institute had long been regarded as the hot-bed of sedition: that Beriah Green, the principal, had been active and successful in propagating the doctrines of abolitionism; that the students, with their principal at their head, had exerted a political influence, and exercised the elective franchise in opposition to the

108 Beriah Green, *Four Sermons* (Cleveland: Herald Office, 1833).
109 Block, "Beriah Green the Reformer," p. 17.
110 Green to Gerrit Smith, 24 September 1835, GSMC.

"republican" party; and that a regard for the stand on the subject of abolitionism, taken by the President of the United States [Andrew Jackson] justified the legislature of this state in withdrawing support from any such institution as the Oneida Institute.[111]

Green believed correctly that he and the other abolitionists had been assailed by men high in authority, who charged "us without a particle of evidence with grave and hateful offences . . . . And for what?", he asked. "For the purpose of preparing the public mind to regard us as outlaws."[112] On 27 April 1836 more than cne hundred fifty people met to protest Senator Wager's policy, adopting resolutions demanding academic freedom.[113] The protest was effective, inasmuch as no legislative action followed Wager's proposal. But in 1839, the struggling institute, whose president's salary was generally months in arrears, was deprived of funds supplied by the American Educational Society. The society discontinued its annual contributions because it alleged the institute had "deficiencies in classical training"![114]

Green, at Oneida, did find himself in an area recently "burned-over" by Charles Grandison Finney, and which was still feeling the effects. In 1836, the Oneida Presbytery stated:

[111] From a printed circular issued by Beriah Green, GSMC. In December 1835 President Jackson, in his message to Congress, assailed the character and designs of the antislavery movement, accusing the abolitionists of circulating through the mails "inflammatory appeals addressed to the passions of the slaves, and calculated to stimulate them to insurrection and all the horrors of civil war;" and the President suggested to Congress a law forbidding the circulation through the mails of incendiary documents.

[112] Ibid.

[113] Harlow, *Gerrit Smith: Philanthropist and Reformer,* p. 225.

[114] Block, "Beriah Green the Reformer," p. 58. While Oneida had some unusual policies about teaching classical languages, these preceded the institute's abolitionist orientation.

The firm and unflinching friends of our oppressed and down trodden country men are increasing in number; and in their attachment to the cause of sacred freedom; and are becoming more and more convinced of the sins and wrongs of American Slavery. . . . In many of the churches the concert of prayer for the abolition of slavery is observed with a deep and lively interest.[115]

But in July of the same year, Green, in response to severe criticism for his abolitionist views from conservative clergy in the area, asked "And we preachers of the gospel, in the midst of these abominations, must close eyes, ears and lips and keep to our proper business of saving souls?"[116]

As a consequence of opposition and suffering brought on by activity based upon his abolitionist ideals, Green's attitude toward the uncommitted, as well as toward the oppressors, grew increasingly hostile. By 1839 his "interpretation of Calvinism proved to be so radically different from that of surrounding clergy that one after another of the orthodox pulpits were closed to him."[117] The abolitionist faction in the community was forced to establish a Congregational church of its own of which Green was pastor from 1843 to 1867. He believed that

good and true men among us must insist upon a reformation in our churches. The-form-of-godliness without the power must be exposed and denounced and abandoned. We must regard in all our aims and exertion—the spirit of the Gospel as the very soul of our designs;—or we can effect nothing for the welfare of the oppressed.[118]

---

[115] *Records of the Oneida Presbytery*, vol. 6, pp. 748–749, quoted in Block, "Beriah Green the Reformer," p. 60.

[116] Beriah Green, "A Letter to a Minister of the Gospel," *Quarterly Anti-Slavery Magazine* 1 (July 1836): 338–339.

[117] Waterman, "Beriah Green," p. 540.

[118] Letter, Beriah Green to Gerrit Smith, 11 July 1841, GSMC.

It was the oppressed with whom Beriah Green identified and to whom he had finally committed his life. Converted by Weld in 1832, Green, in a high status position, took his first risk on behalf of the slave in that year, challenging the trustees of Western Reserve College. As a consequence, he suffered, and his resonance to abolitionism increased; as a result his willingness to take risks did the same. He was soon suffering again under an attack by a state senator and threatened with the loss of funds. His institute did suffer an actual loss of financial support in 1839. Each step of the way there was an increase in resonance to antislavery, an increased hostility toward the oppressor and toward those who remained uncommitted.

Green was not unaware of this process: " 'Oppression maketh a wise man mad.' A little of the inconveniency of madness must be expected and borne with. We are so formed, moreover, and so affected often, that we too easily slide into the temper and conduct, which we most condemn in others."[119]

William Goodell

William Goodell was born on 25 October 1792 in Coventry, Chenango County, New York, where his parents, Frederic and Rhoda (Guernsey) Goodell lived "a pioneer life of great privation and hardship."[120]

The future editor was a child of delicate health; he was forced to spend much time indoors where his mother encouraged his interest in literature, especially religious writings, with which her library was filled.[121] William's "parents were

[119] Beriah Green to Theodore Dwight Weld, 14 April 1839, Weld Collection, Library of Congress.
[120] [Lavinia Goodell], *In Memoriam: William Goodell* (Chicago: Guilbert & Winchell, 1879), p. 4.
[121] Ibid., p. 6.

both devoted Christians, and he dated his own conversion from his seventh year."[122] Methodist circuits were early established in this frontier area of Chenango, and a religious class or study group was formed by the residents. Frederic Goodell and his wife were among the first members.[123]

When William was eleven, his mother died and he was sent to Amenia, New York, to live with his uncle. There he attended common school and assisted with the light farm work. In 1805 he went to live with his grandmother in Pomfret, Connecticut. Mrs. Goodell was a "strong-minded woman with advanced ideas on some of the social evils of her day."[124] She apparently played an important role in William's moral and intellectual development, for "among his most valued literary and religious privileges he numbered the society of his grandmother."[125]

William Goodell spent five years in Connecticut attending common school winters and working on his grandmother's farm summers. He attended the Congregational church during this time and enjoyed the "advantages of two good libraries."[126] Meanwhile, the elder Goodell died in 1806.

Young William longed for a college education, but lack of funds prevented the fulfillment of this hope, and at the age of eighteen he accepted a mercantile opening in Providence, Rhode Island. Two years later he was an officer among the "cadets" training for possible military duty in the War of 1812. And in 1815 "he appears to have been in business for himself."[127] Between 1817 and 1819 he was supercargo on a

122 Ibid., p. 7.
123 Ibid.
124 W. Randall Waterman, "William Goodell," *Dictionary of American Biography*, ed. by Allen Johnson, vol. 7 (New York: Charles Scribner's Sons, 1931), p. 384.
125 [Lavinia Goodell], *In Memoriam*, p. 11.
126 Waterman, "William Goodell," p. 384.
127 [Lavinia Goodell], *In Memoriam*, p. 13.

ship owned by Butler, Carrington and Company, traders with the Orient. In this capacity William went on "long, but prosperous and instructive voyages."[128]

In 1819 Goodell went into partnership with his employer and engaged in the flour trade at Alexandria, Virginia, where he resided for a short time. In 1823, he married Clarissa C. Dady; "he was now a successful merchant, and able to surround himself with comforts and luxuries."[129]

When trade fluctuations causing heavy financial losses and the subsequent death of his partner forced William to give up his business, he entered the employ of Phelps and Peck as a bookkeeper. The ledger book apparently bored him, however, for in 1827 he was editing, full time, a temperance newspaper, the *Weekly Investigator*, in Providence, Rhode Island.

In 1829, the paper was moved to Boston and was merged with the *National Philanthropist;* in 1830, the paper was moved once more—this time to New York as the *Genius of Temperance.* To arouse interest and gain subscriptions, Goodell was frequently forced into the lecture field. In 1833, he helped to organize the American Anti-Slavery Society and began to publish the *Emancipator,* which became in 1834 the Society's official publication.[130]

Goodell's interest in antislavery did not begin only after the failure of his business; as early as 1820 when he was successfully involved in a mercantile partnership he contributed a poem and, subsequently, a series of articles to the *Providence Gazette* that were severely critical of the Missouri Compromise for allowing slavery in a new state.

In 1836, Goodell went to Utica on the urging of the New York State Anti-Slavery Society and the personal invitation of Alvan Stewart, Beriah Green, and Theodore Dwight Weld,

---

[128] Ibid.
[129] Ibid., p. 16.
[130] Waterman, "William Goodell," p. 385.

to take charge of a weekly antislavery paper to be called *Friend of Man.*

After committing himself to abolitionism as a way of life, Goodell was once forced to flee his home in Brooklyn. He and his family sought shelter in an obscure locality of New York until the fury of the mob had spent itself. At another time Goodell barely escaped an angry mob routing an anti-slavery meeting in New York.[131]

Yet Goodell remained nonviolent. He criticized the action of the martyr Elijah Lovejoy who attempted to defend his press and himself by violence against an antiabolitionist mob bent on destruction. Goodell was afraid that abolitionists might arm themselves in self-defense, that bloodshed would inevitably follow, and that the country might then become "a scene of domestic violence in which the abolitionists would be almost certain to be overpowered."[132]

He continued to edit the *Friend of Man* from 1836 to 1842, and in the meantime he lectured widely; in 1840, he helped organize the Liberty party. During this time, he "read elementary law works carefully till he became so well versed in the science that he was urged to apply for admission to the bar."[133] In his newspapers he used legal and political as well as religious arguments in replying to the allegation that it was not safe to emancipate slaves. A claim that the Constitution "can secure *general liberty*," he wrote, "and at the same time guaranty *local slavery,* or even compromise or permit its existence, is to affirm the greatest of moral absurdities, to deny self-evident truths, to falsify human history. . . ."[134]

[131] [Lavinia Goodell], *In Memoriam,* p. 25.

[132] *Liberator,* 6 September 1839. This evidently reflects a pragmatic sort of concern and is therefore to be distinguished from the philosophy of nonresistance.

[133] [Lavinia Goodell], *In Memoriam,* p. 30.

[134] William Goodell, *Views of American Constitutional Law in Its Bearing upon American Slavery* (Utica: Jackson and Chaplin, 1844), p. 11.

In 1843, Goodell was invited to set up in Honeoye, New York, his ideal church, based upon temperance, antislavery, and church union principles. Goodell for a long time believed that even a church neutral on antislavery was "an anti-Christian church" which must be abandoned in order to avoid partaking of its sins.[135] But avoiding sin was not enough for Goodell who continually endeavored to induce churches in complicity with slavery to take action against it.[136] "Reformation," he wrote, "must begin at the house of God. Until THIS work is attempted, all our other attempts at reformation will prove futile."[137]

He wrote extensively on slavery while at Honeoye, and, in 1847, feeling that the Liberty party's insistence on "one-issue politics" was too narrow, he helped organize the Liberty League which took positions on slavery, tariffs, land monopoly, and war among other issues.

Goodell continually evidenced his desire for the literal attainment of his objective. In 1862, he wrote to his wife from Washington, telling of a meeting he had had with President Lincoln in which the abolitionist recommended emancipation. Shortly before the Emancipation Proclamation was issued, Goodell again talked to Lincoln and reported later that he had the satisfaction of seeing some of his own phrases incorporated in the document.[138]

He did not drop his pen with emancipation, but wielded it against intemperance and the exclusion of women from the suffrage, among other social issues. Raised in an actively religious household, exposed to a grandmother who was outspoken on social evils, Goodell was interested in antislavery

135 William Goodell, *Come-Outerism: The Duty of Secession from a Corrupt Church* (New York: American Anti-Slavery Society, 1845), pp. 22–25.

136 [Lavinia Goodell], *In Memoriam*, p. 27.

137 Quoted in Ibid., p. 29.

138 Henderson, "History of New York State Anti-Slavery Society," p. 388.

early. By 1833, he had aligned himself with the abolitionists. After emancipation he interested himself in other social reforms. He was "ever hopeful for the future, having a firm faith in the coming of that day when 'the kingdoms of this world shall become the kingdom of our Lord and of his Christ.' "[139]

[139] [Lavinia Goodell], *In Memoriam,* p. 33.

3

Ten High-Ranking New York Abolitionist Leaders

Henry Brewster Stanton

HENRY B. STANTON, one of the most effective administrative officers in the antislavery movement, was born in Griswold, Connecticut, on 27 June 1805. His father, Joseph, a woolen manufacturer and merchant, traced his ancestry to emigrants from England in the 1630s. Henry's mother, Susan Brewster, was a descendent of William Brewster who arrived in 1620.[1]

After studying at the Jewett City Academy in Connecticut, Henry, "handsome, personal[ly] charm[ing]," went to Rochester in 1826 to write for Thurlow Weed's *Monroe Telegraph* and to work as a clerk in the canal office in that city. In 1828

[1] "Henry Brewster Stanton," *Appleton's Cyclopedia*, ed. by J. G. Wilson and John Fiske, vol. 5 (New York: D. Appleton and Co., 1888), p. 649.

he wrote for the *Telegraph* on behalf of John Quincy Adams.[2] The next year he became deputy clerk of Monroe County, New York, continuing in that office while supplying "deficiencies in an imperfect education" by studying law and the classics until 1832.[3]

In October 1830, Charles Grandison Finney, the most famous evangelist of the era, came to Rochester to supply the pulpit of the Third Presbyterian Church. Henry was asked to hear him:

> I listened. It did not sound like preaching, but like a lawyer arguing a case before a court and jury. . . . The discourse was a chain of logic. . . . I have heard many celebrated pulpit orators in various parts of the world. Taken all in all, I never knew the superior of Charles G. Finney.[4]

Finney regarded his success at Rochester as among the greatest of his remarkable career. In any case, he converted Henry Brewster Stanton. Immediately subsequent to this experience, Stanton came into contact with Theodore Dwight Weld, and in spring 1832 went to Lane Theological Seminary near Cincinnati.[5]

In summer 1832 the following question was debated by the debate club at the seminary: "If the slaves of the South were to rise in insurrection, would it be the duty of the North to aid in putting it down?" Everyone in the club placed himself on the affirmative side of the room except Henry B. Stanton. He made his first antislavery speech, but not his last. It was

2 Mary W. Williams, "Henry Brewster Stanton," *Dictionary of American Biography,* ed. by Allen Johnson, vol. 18 (New York: Charles Scribner's Sons, 1936), p. 524.

3 Henry Brewster Stanton, *Random Recollections* (Johnstown, N.Y.: Blunck and Leaning, 1885), p. 43.

4 Ibid., p. 41.

5 Williams, "Henry Brewster Stanton," p. 525.

also not the last time he was to stand alone in the midst of opposition.[6]

Weld took his place with the students at Lane about this time and began laying the ground for a major discussion on slavery. The Lane Debate, when it came, brought together all the students and most of the faculty. Nine days of discussion led by Weld resulted in an overwhelming affirmative vote on the question: "Ought the people of the slave-holding states to abolish slavery immediately?" In two years Weld had brought about the most strategic act of his abolitionist career.[7]

In fall 1834 Stanton helped in the organization of an Anti-Slavery Society at Lane, and the students set up an intensive program for aiding Negroes. The trustees, who tried to prevent all discussion of the slavery question, and who argued that "education must be completed before the young are fitted to engage in the collisions of active life,"[8] opposed the society and in consequence Stanton left the seminary, joined by about fifty other students.[9] Henry at once associated himself with James G. Birney in his antislavery work.

In the next twelve years he was on the executive committee of the American Anti-Slavery Society, and as secretary addressed many legislative commissions and made platform speeches from Maine to Indiana. During one of his earliest speeches at a small meeting at Newport, Rhode Island, in 1835, a mob "of respectable size . . . stoned the building, smashed the windows," and drove the antislavery people into the street.[10]

In 1836, he was "outrageously treated while attempting to

[6] Stanton, *Random Recollections*, p. 47.

[7] Louis Filler, *The Crusade Against Slavery* (New York: Harper and Bros., 1960), p. 69.

[8] Robert Fletcher, *History of Oberlin College* (Oberlin: Oberlin Press, 1943), vol. 1, p. 150ff.

[9] *Liberator*, 10 January 1835.

[10] Stanton, *Random Recollections*, p. 52.

speak to a meeting in a Methodist Church at Providence."[11] After delivering an address at a church in Livingston County in 1837, Stanton discovered the next morning that the building had been burned by antiabolitionist conservatives.[12] It was not the last time that Stanton was to meet both verbal and physical abuse in an attempt to fulfill the goals he had begun to formulate in 1832.

During these years of personal confrontation with violence and suffering at the hands of antiabolitionists, Stanton's identification with the oppressed increased, as did his commitment to the cause of antislavery. He made a phenomenal number of speeches, collected thousands of dollars for the Anti-Slavery Society, and effectively managed the petition campaign of antislavery men. His activities were not without some victories: "We have had a triumph," he wrote Smith in 1840; "The Whig . . . candidates . . . spent weeks and hundreds to carry their point. . . . Their whole ticket is defeated. . . . Ah me! Our cause goes slowly—but it *shall* prevail."[13]

This continuing alternation between opposition, violence, and suffering, and the partial victories with the rising expectations they induced deepened Stanton's commitment and gradually made it appear that the cause was what he had been born for. Stanton wrote: "I feel that the honor and in some measure the prosperity of the antislavery cause in this country is committed to us. . . . I have pledged myself to the deliverance of the poor captive, and God giving me grace, I will redeem the pledge."[14]

Stanton married Elizabeth Cady on 10 May 1840 about whom he had written to Smith three months earlier: "It pains me to see a person of so superior a mind and enlarged heart

11 Ibid.
12 Ibid., p. 53.
13 Stanton to Gerrit Smith, n.d. 1840, GSMC.
14 Stanton to Gerrit Smith, 10 April 1840, GSMC.

doing nothing for a wicked world's salvation."[15] Exposed to Henry's personal charm, eloquence, and religiosity, however, Elizabeth was soon imbued with the reform spirit. Just after their marriage, they sailed to London to attend the World Anti-Slavery Convention to which Henry was a delegate.

Upon his return to America, he studied law with his father-in-law, was admitted to the bar, and began practicing.[16] "He was successful at the law, but his continued interest in abolition led him into increased political activity."[17] Here opposition continued: "We have had everything to contend with. . . . The coalition between the Clay-Whigs and the non-voting and the voting Garrisonians was open and shameless. . . . Now we are to be set upon by Native-Americanism."[18] Despite opposition Stanton was generally popular. In 1849 and 1851 he was elected to the state senate from Seneca Falls.

Converted by Finney during his Rochester revival, the popular, handsome, and eloquent Stanton soon after was attracted to abolitionism. His attachment to the cause probably increased after his exposure to Weld, and Stanton's first risk on behalf of the slave initiated for him a cycle of punishment —"his . . . denunciations subjected him . . . to scores of mob attacks"[19]—increased resonance, and increased commitment.

15 Stanton to Smith, 27 February 1840, GSMC.
16 Williams, "Henry Brewster Stanton," p. 525. In 1847 Stanton entered into partnership with Horace E. Smith, one of New York State's top one hundred abolitionist leaders. Smith was admitted to the Supreme Courts of New York State and of the United States in the 1840s. He was an elder in the Presbyterian church for many years, a member of the Massachusetts legislature from 1851–1852, and the dean of the Albany Law School.
17 Williams, "Henry Brewster Stanton," p. 525.
18 Stanton to Gerrit Smith, 12 November 1844, GSMC.
19 Williams, "Henry Brewster Stanton," p. 525.

Joshua Leavitt

The abolitionist Joshua Leavitt who, according to Theodore Dwight Weld, had in the 1830s "more actual influence over the giving, doing, daring, praying and accomplishing part of the church than any other man,"[20] was born on 8 September 1794 in Heath, Franklin County, Massachusetts.

Leavitt was interested in reform early; as an undergraduate at Yale, he organized the Yale College Benevolent Society which from 1813 on attracted pious youths wishing to aid their fellow man.[21] After being graduated from Yale in 1814, Joshua Leavitt studied law and was admitted to the bar in 1819. In the same year he organized one of the first Sabbath schools in Heath. He began practicing law in Putney, Vermont, but by 1823 he was studying theology, and in 1825 was graduated from the Yale Divinity School.[22]

Between 1825 and 1828 Leavitt was in charge of a Congregational church at Stratford, Connecticut, during which time he entered upon a strenuous round of missionary and reforming activities, including lectures for the American Temperance Society. He wrote articles about slavery for the *Christian Spectator,* and contributed to the *Journal of Public Morals* in this first phase of his career.[23]

It was in editing religious and quasi-religious journals that Joshua Leavitt made his mark. Weld, in fact, believed that Leavitt had "revolutionized the character of the religious periodical press." In 1831, he published the *Evangelist,* doc-

[20] Theodore Dwight Weld to James G. Birney, 26 June 1837, *Letters of James G. Birney, 1831–1857,* vol. 1, ed. by Dwight Dumond (New York: Appleton-Century Co., 1938), p. 390.

[21] Charles C. Cole, *The Social Ideas of Northern Evangelists* (New York: Columbia University Press, 1954), p. 40.

[22] "Joshua Leavitt," *Appleton's Cyclopedia,* ed. by J. G. Wilson and John Fiske, vol. 3 (New York: D. Appleton and Co., 1888), p. 649.

[23] Filler, *The Crusade Against Slavery,* p. 24.

trinally associated with the New School faction, and fostering temperance, religious revivals and antislavery.[24] While Leavitt devoted more space in the *Evangelist* to other things than slavery, it was his preaching on this subject which ate into the paper's circulation, and which forced Leavitt to flee several times between 1833 and 1835 to escape mob violence.[25] It took a series of revival lectures by Charles G. Finney in 1834 to restore the paper's circulation, which reached 10,000 subscribers by 1837.

Leavitt, in between fleeing pursuers, wrote to Gerrit Smith in 1834 about the Colonization Society in which he had lost interest because of an increasing commitment to abolitionism: "I do not believe you will long continue to waste your sympathy or your liberality upon an institution of so little good, and so much evil." Leavitt's commitment to abolitionism and the free black was so intense by 1834 that he not only wanted to discontinue colonization, but suggested bringing the exiles back "to their own native country and to the privileges of schools, of the gospel, and of a well regulated government."[26]

In 1837, despite the fact that the circulation of the *Evangelist* had reached its peak, the depression forced Leavitt to give it up. He soon acted on his ever increasing commitment to abolitionism, however, by taking up the editorship of the *Emancipator,* a paper he personally turned into the leading organ for the expression of political abolitionism. He moved the paper in 1842 to Boston, where he carried on the anti-slavery cause as well as the campaign for cheap postage, free trade, and temperance.[27]

Prior to this, however, in early 1841, with financial assistance

24 Cole, *The Social Ideas of Northern Evangelists,* p. 40.

25 "Joshua Leavitt," p. 649.

26 Joshua Leavitt to Gerrit Smith, 31 March 1834, GSMC.

27 Frank W. Coburn, "Joshua Leavitt," *Dictionary of American Biography,* ed. by Allen Johnson, vol. 11 (New York: Charles Scribner's Sons, 1933), p. 85.

from Lewis Tappan, Leavitt went to Washington to cover the
congressional session for the *Emancipator* and to work in the
antislavery petition fight then raging in the House of Representatives,[28] serving mainly as a gadfly to antislavery Whig
congressmen. Leavitt was early interested in moving abolitionism into the political arena, and was one of the founders
of the Liberty party. As a leader of this newly formed organization, "Leavitt was impatient with antislavery politicians who
remained in the Whig Party and who seemed sometimes to
subordinate the slavery question to political expediency."[29]

Leavitt had begun as early as 1839 to criticize Congressman
Seth Gates[30] and others like him "who feel and act on the
ground that . . . paltry matters . . . are more important than
the great question of *Human Freedom.*" These, he said, "can
have but small interest in the antislavery cause."[31] Leavitt's
perseverance in criticism was not rhetorical flourish, or necessarily motivated by a need to reduce tension, for his continued nagging was not without effect. In autumn 1841, a
"little group of antislavery Whigs [including Congressman
Gates] decided to form an insurgent band to carry on guerilla
warfare in Congress against slavery."[32]

Despite these major accomplishments, Leavitt often con-

[28] James McPherson, "Fight Against the Gag Rule," *Journal of Negro
History* 48 (July 1963): 180.

[29] Ibid., p. 181.

[30] Seth Gates (1800–1877), antislavery Whig congressman, 1839–1843, a
Weld convert, one of New York's top one hundred abolitionist leaders,
did contemplate joining the Liberty party but explained to Birney in
1839, "I cannot, however, get along with all their views and positions, and
so I hold on where I am, receiving all the curses of the South for my
ultra abolitionism, and the cuffs of the third party men of the North,
for my Whigism." After receiving the stinging criticism of Joshua
Leavitt and having been mobbed twice in his home town, Gates led the
antislavery Whigs in Congress more intensely against proslavery measures
(Gates to Birney, *Letters of James G. Birney, 1831–1857*, vol. 2, p. 196).

[31] *Emancipator*, 10 October 1839.

[32] *Emanicipator*, 10 June 1841.

sidered himself a failure. He was relatively poor all his life and seems to have brooded about this a good deal.[33] There is, moreover, some evidence that Leavitt was sometimes quick to accuse friends and enemies alike of wrongdoing because they happened to disagree with him.[34]

His sharp mind, however, allowed him to cut quickly through irrelevancies and penetrate to the core of a problem. And his constant accusations often paid off in literal attainment of his objectives such as goading the antislavery Whigs into action and later in 1848 forcing the Free Soil party leaders to make slavery an open issue.[35]

Leavitt represented that blend of high idealism and practicality that constantly reinvigorated the abolitionist movement. He believed that slavery could be abolished under the Constitution. One of his critics has written about Joshua Leavitt: "Ever sincere, he desired to persuade the public that abolitionism was a logical, sensible, respectable idea, and felt that the cause would not be helped 'by twaddle.' "[36]

Lewis Tappan

Lewis Tappan was born 23 May 1788 in Northampton, Massachusetts, and grew up along with his brother Arthur[37] and

[33] See for examples: Joshua Leavitt to Mrs. Leavitt, 17 January 1835, Joshua Leavitt to Hooker Leavitt, 21 November 1840 and 7 December 1847, Leavitt Papers, Library of Congress.

[34] McPherson, "Fight Against the Gag Rule," p. 180.

[35] Barnes, *The Antislavery Impulse*, p. 46.

[36] Cole, *Social Ideas of Northern Evangelists*, p. 202.

[37] Arthur Tappan (1786–1865) was a leading merchant in New York City. He served as president or executive officer of the American Sunday School Union, American Bible Society, American Tract Society, Union Missionary Society, New York Evangelical Society of Missions, American Education Society, New York Magdalen Society, and the General Union for Promoting the Observance of the Christian Sabbath. Despite Arthur's

nine other siblings in the strictly religious household of
Benjamin and Sarah (Homes) Tappan.

There was nothing "particularly insecure or hostile in the
social climate of Northampton which could account in any
way for Lewis Tappan's later deviation from the path of a
typical New England merchant. His mother and father gave
all the children a wholesome home life" and their river town
was "sleepy, conservative and safe."[38]

Benjamin Tappan was of French origin, descended from
the Huguenots, and owned a dry goods business in Northampton. Lewis's father rather mystified his son by his lack of
personal ambition; he was "seemingly content to make an
honest living," his annual income never exceeding $1,000.[39]

Lewis was educated in the town school and in 1804, at the
age of sixteen, was apprenticed as a clerk to a dry goods im-
porting firm in Boston.[40] Here he met Susan Aspinwall whom
he married in 1813. The marriage represented for Lewis a
climb from rural obscurity to metropolitan distinction. It was
in Boston as well that he came under the influence of the
famous Unitarian minister, William Ellery Channing, and
served in 1825 as treasurer of the American Unitarian Association. By 1828, however, he was writing pamphlets upholding
his earlier evangelical convictions against Unitarianism.[41]

---

prominence in the benevolent system, one gets the impression that most
of the momentum in the joint endeavors of the two brothers was due to
Lewis Tappan, whose habit was to do the work and give the credit to
Arthur (see *Letters of T. D. Weld*, ed. by Gilbert Hobbs Barnes and
Dwight Dumond, vol. 1. [Gloucester: Peter Smith, 1965], p. 100). Moreover, after the crisis of 1837, Arthur Tappan's active participation in the
antislavery movement largely ceased.

38 Bertram Wyatt-Brown, *Lewis Tappan* (Cleveland: Case Western
Reserve University Press, 1969), p. 2.

39 Lewis Tappan, "Autobiography," pp. 3, 19, 20, handwritten, Tappan
Collection, Library of Congress.

40 Ibid., p. 51.

41 Frank J. Klingberg, "Lewis Tappan," *Dictionary of American
Biography*, ed. by Allen Johnson, vol. 18 (New York: Charles Scribner's
Sons, 1936), p. 303.

In 1828 Lewis Tappan entered into partnership with his brother Arthur as a silk jobber in New York. As credit manager of Arthur Tappan and Company, Lewis was a significant factor in the prosperity of the firm in the years preceding the depression of 1837.[42] In 1841, after withdrawing from the partnership, he established under "The Mercantile Agency," the firm name of Lewis Tappan and Company, the first commercial credit rating agency in the country. He successfully managed this enterprise until 1849, when he retired to devote himself to benevolent work, which had become his chief concern.[43]

During 1830 Charles Grandison Finney preached the "Great Revival" in New York City, and the Tappan brothers fell under his influence. During Finney's stay, they founded the *New York Evangelist* to publish his views and to spread the "Great Revival" throughout the nation. Lewis and Arthur were also instrumental in building the Broadway Tabernacle for the great evangelist.[44] Finney reinforced religious impulses that were already stirring the Tappans, for as soon as they began to accumulate wealth in 1828 they began to "reflect seriously upon [their] obligations as . . . steward[s] of the lord."[45] And from the time of his first business success, Lewis was a supporter of the American Board of Commissioners for Foreign Missions and the American Bible Society. Whenever

42 Ibid.
43 Ibid.
44 Ibid.
45 Lewis Tappan, *Life of Arthur Tappan* (New York: Hurd and Houghton, 1870), p. 62. The brothers had also formed an "Association of Gentlemen" made up in the main of merchants dedicated to Christian good works. Others of the top one hundred abolitionist leaders in New York who were members of the association were John Rankin, a merchant associate of the Tappans who had helped found the *New York Evangelist*, and who participated in the organization of the New York City Anti-Slavery Society, and William Green, Jr. (1796–1881), also a New York merchant who was a founder of the New York City Anti-Slavery Society and the American Anti-Slavery Society. Green also helped finance the Second Free Presbyterian Church.

Theodore Dwight Weld was in New York City, he and Tappan had long conversations. "It was during these sessions that Tappan came to understand immediate abolitionism."[46]

Lewis Tappan in 1833, already phenomenally successful in business and held in high regard by his contemporaries, helped found the New York Anti-Slavery Society and the American Anti-Slavery Society. On 4 July 1834 "a pillaging crowd in a holiday mood, sacked the house of Lewis Tappan, burning his furniture in the streets. Not even his children's toys were spared."[47] Seven days later crowds attacked the First Free Presbyterian Church which Tappan had helped organize, as well as the church of Samuel H. Cox[48] and two Negro worship halls.

Lewis Tappan wrote to Weld in reference to the attack upon his property: "It is my wish that my house may remain this summer as it is, a silent anti-slavery preacher to the crowds who will flock to see it. . . . I hope not to be proud of the distinction conferred upon me. It has been my honest endeavor to do my duty. . . . I have contended earnestly for the doctrines of Immediate Emancipation and still mean to do it come what will to my person, property or reputation. The cause is a righteous one. It is I believe dear to the heart of the Savior. Shall we then, like recreants, abandon it?

46 Wyatt-Brown, *Lewis Tappan*, p. 100.
47 Charles C. Cole, "The Free Church Movement in New York City," *New York History* 34 (July 1953): 284–297.
48 Samuel Hanson Cox (1793–1881), one of the top one hundred abolitionist leaders in New York, was pastor of the Laight Street Church from 1825–1835. His congregation consisted mainly of wealthy merchants. Cox said in 1834, "Emancipation is too limited. . . . What I ask for our colored brethren is that they should be immediately admitted to share with us in the blessings of equal citizenship" (*First Annual Report of the American Anti-Slavery Society* [New York: American Anti-Slavery Society, 1834], p. 6).
In addition to the attack on his church, Cox's house was stoned, and in July 1835 he was hanged in effigy in Charleston, South Carolina.

Forbid it philanthropy, forbid it religion! 'We cannot but speak the things which we have seen and heard.' "[49] In summer 1835, Lewis's brother Arthur Tappan received letters threatening him with assassination. Later that year the construction of the Tappans' Tabernacle Church which was to be racially integrated aroused rumors of amalgamation, and before it was completed the building was set on fire.

Lewis Tappan, raised in a strictly religious household from 1788–1804, aroused by Charles G. Finney in 1830, and influenced after that by Theodore Dwight Weld, took his first risk on behalf of the oppressed black in 1833. As a consequence, punishment and suffering were inflicted upon him throughout 1834 and 1835.

Tappan's commitment to abolitionism and the cause of the free black increased. Early in 1836, Lewis and Arthur withdrew their financial support from Oberlin College because they thought even Finney, for whom they had established a professorship at the school, was shirking on the subject of antislavery.[50] In the same year Lewis Tappan "thought that the 'negro pew' should be done away. . . . Finding nothing could be done in a matter so dear to my heart, I left the church."[51] On 9 March 1836 when abolitionist leaders of the American Anti-Slavery Society met in New York, Lewis Tappan proposed that a Negro minister be invited to deliver one of the addresses. Considerable opposition, however, thwarted the plan.[52] Thus Tappan met opposition not only from anti-

---

[49] Lewis Tappan to Weld, 10 July 1834, *Letters of Theodore Dwight Weld*, vol. 1, p. 153.

[50] Lewis Tappan, diary, 19 March 1836, pp. 17–18, Tappan Collection, Library of Congress.

[51] Quoted in Cole, "The Free Church Movement in New York City," p. 295.

[52] Lewis Tappan to Weld, 15 March 1836, in *Letters of Theodore Dwight Weld, Angelina Grimké Weld, and Sarah Grimké, 1822–1844*, ed. by G. H. Barnes and Dwight Dumond, vol. 1 (New York: Appleton-Cen-

abolitionists but from antislavery men not as committed as he.

Yet as late as 1839 Lewis Tappan continued to take the position that abolitionists would lose their influence as moral reformers if they participated in the self-seeking arena of politics. If the abolitionists organized a third party, Tappan thought, many might conclude that abolitionists had lost confidence in God's power to free the slave.[53] Tappan should not be considered on this account, however, a nonresistance Garrisonian. Tappan perceived the importance of uniting the Garrisonians and the so-called respectable element of the abolitionist movement. And for a while he served as the bridge between them; but he split with William Lloyd Garrison in 1840, as did the greatest part of the antislavery movement, because Garrison, Tappan believed, "avowed . . . that there were subjects [no-government, women's rights] paramount to the Anti-Slavery Cause. And he was using the Society as an instrument to establish these notions."[54]

Moreover, with the increase in the intransigence and hostility of antiabolitionists, Tappan came to favor more and more radical methods of action. Joseph Sturge, the leader of the British antislavery movement, in conversation with Lewis convinced the American to look more favorably upon the

---

tury, 1934), pp. 276–277. It is true that many abolitionists shared the ideas of race held by the majority of their contemporaries in the core society. On this point see Leon Litwack, *North of Slavery* (Chicago: University of Chicago Press, 1961); William Stanton, *The Leopard's Spots: Scientific Attitudes Toward Race in America, 1815–1859* (Chicago: University of Chicago Press, 1960).

It is to the credit of those abolitionists who believed in black inferiority that they transcended this idea and advocated emancipation if not social equality. More important, the great majority of high ranking abolitionist leaders in New York State, including Lewis Tappan, appear to have come to believe in and act for complete black equality. This idea will be developed further in chapters 2–4.

[53] *Friend of Man*, 4 December 1839.

[54] Lewis Tappan to Weld, 26 May 1840, Tappan Collection, Library of Congress.

Liberty party. Even after Tappan joined the political abolitionists, he doubted Liberty men would stay "true to their
principles."[55] He gradually adopted the view that slavery was
illegal everywhere and could be abolished by the federal
government in the slave states under the Constitution. And
after the passage of the Fugitive Slave Act in 1850, Lewis
Tappan became a supporter of those who urged Christians to
disobey it.[56]

Lewis Tappan, eminently successful, extremely wealthy
"merchant prince" of New York City, experienced no "elbow-
ing aside" by new groups rising to ascendency in the American
social and economic hierarchy, and thus experienced no status
frustration. His first experience with significant frustration
came only after he took his first risk on behalf of oppressed
blacks. The risk was taken out of a resonance and growing
commitment to abolitionism—a resonance induced by an
evangelical upbringing and a commitment reinforced by the
preaching of Charles G. Finney and the persistence of
Theodore Dwight Weld. The commitment was sealed by
violent opposition.

William Jay

William Jay was born in New York City 16 June 1789, the
son of John Jay and Sarah Van Brugh Livingston. John Jay,
active in the public life of the United States of America for
thirty years, holding among other offices that of Chief Justice
of the United States Supreme Court and Governor of New
York, provided a model which predisposed his sons, Peter
Augustus and William, to resonate to movements based on

---

[55] Lewis Tappan to Seth Gates, 21 October 1843, letterbook, Tappan
Collection, Library of Congress.
[56] Wyatt-Brown, *Lewis Tappan*, p. 319.

public service. The father's abolitionist sentiments and activities, moreover, made it more likely that the sons would also be attracted to antislavery.[57] As Horace Greeley wrote:

> As to Chief Justice Jay, the father, may be attributed, more than to any other man, the abolition of negro bondage in this state [New York], so to Judge William Jay, the son, the future will give the credit of having been one of the earliest advocates of the modern anti-slavery movements, which at this moment influence so radically the religion and the philanthropy of the country.[58]

Following a classical training under Thomas Ellison, rector of St. Peter's Church in Albany, and college preparation under Henry Davis, future president of Hamilton College, William Jay entered Yale in 1804. He was graduated there in 1808 and studied law with John B. Henry of Albany. Impaired eyesight prevented active practice, however, and he turned to agricultural pursuits on his father's eight hundred acres at Bedford.[59]

In 1812, William married Augusta McVickar, daughter of a New York merchant. Three years later he published "Memoir on the Subject of a General Bible Society for the United States," and in 1816, assisted Elias Boudinot and others in forming the American Bible Society. For many years Jay was the society's most active and practical promoter.[60]

Governor DeWitt Clinton appointed Jay to the bench of Westchester County in 1818. He held this post until 1843 when

[57] A. E. Peterson, "William Jay," *Dictionary of American Biography,* ed. by Allen Johnson, vol. 10 (New York: Charles Scribner's Sons, 1933), p. 11.

[58] Quoted in John Jay, "William Jay," *Appleton's Cyclopedia,* ed. by J. G. Wilson and John Fiske, vol. 3 (New York: D. Appleton and Co., 1888), p. 413.

[59] Bayard Tuckerman, *William Jay and the Constitutional Movement for the Abolition of Slavery* (New York: Dodd, Mead and Co., 1893), p. 10.

[60] Ibid., p. 13.

he was removed through the influence of proslavery Democrats. This was not the first time William Jay suffered at the hands of antiabolitionists, for he had been active in antislavery since at least as early as 1819 when during the Missouri Controversy he had written strongly against the extension of slavery, demanding that Congress should "stand between the living and the dead, and stay the plague."[61]

In 1826 Jay was instrumental in calling the attention of the New York legislature and of Congress to the necessity of reforming the slave laws of the District of Columbia. In May 1833, the first number of the *Emancipator* had a contribution from Judge Jay. He opposed colonization, declaring that those who favored the plan were not moved by "the precepts of the Gospel" but by "prejudice."[62]

Although Jay had been an earnest emancipationist since 1824, he had had doubts about the efficacy of organizing antislavery societies even at so late a period in the movement as 1834.[63] In 1834, however, mobs of antiabolitionists in New York City, accusing the antislavery people of amalgamationism and fanaticism, destroyed the property of antislavery leaders and went on a rampage of violence through the Negro districts of the city. Immediately after the riots, William Jay took a place on the Executive Committee of the American Anti-Slavery Society.[64] In William Jay, given his developing commitment to antislavery, these events probably aroused vicarious distress, shame, fear or sympathy for the victims of the violence, and anger or contempt for the aggressors. As a by-product, the idea of the victim, i.e., abolitionism, tended to

61 Jay, "William Jay," p. 411.
62 William Jay, *An Inquiry into the Character and Tendency of the American Colonization and American Anti-Slavery Societies* (New York: Leavitt, Lord and Co., 1835), passim.
63 Tuckerman, *William Jay*, p. 57.
64 Linda K. Kerber, "Abolitionists and Amalgamators: The New York City Race Riots of 1834," *New York History* 48 (January 1967): 28–40.

have more influence upon Jay than before the attack in 1834.

Despite his increased commitment, there was about Jay little of the intemperate agitator; it was his notion that emancipation be urged with the Constitution in hand.[65] Like so many of the abolitionist leaders, Jay had legal training,[66] and thus could speak the language of the law as well as the Bible. His voice was often raised in the interest of legality and moderation, as he preferred efficiency (i.e., literal attainment of the ideal) to rhetoric (i.e., "action").[67] In keeping with his newly intensified commitment, Jay published in 1837 *A View of the Action of the Federal Government in Behalf of Slavery* wherein this son of an outstanding founding father could question the value of the American union if it be a union for "the destruction of liberty," a national compact "enforced by gag laws, a censorship of the press, and the abrogation of the right of petition."[68] In no way, however, could this be interpreted as unpatriotic. It was the antiabolitionists, after all, who were willing to toss out civil liberties with the bath water of emancipation; William Jay and the abolitionists, on the other hand, fought to preserve these liberties as the best part of the American heritage.

In 1840 William Jay declined the gubernatorial nomination of the Liberty party because he did not approve "under present circumstances of any further organized interference by abolitionists with elections than the official questioning of candidates."[69] Yet by 1843, after being exposed to "the fury of proslavery Drunken vagabonds",[70] and as both major parties continued to seem irrevocably pledged to the support of

---

65 Tuckerman, *William Jay*, p. 16.

66 See chapter 4.

67 Kerber, "Abolitionists and Amalgamators," p. 37.

68 William Jay, *A View of the Action of the Federal Government in Behalf of Slavery* (New York: J. S. Taylor, 1839), p. 93.

69 Jay to Gerrit Smith, July 1840, cited in Tuckerman, *William Jay*, p. 111.

70 Jay to Gerrit Smith, 8 September 1843, GSMC.

slavery, Jay became a pronounced and active member of the Liberty party.[71] "I deliberated long," wrote Jay, "and finally came to the conclusion that *if* my name was required for the good of the cause, I ought not to withold it."[72]

It is obvious that the pathway from early resonance, induced by a model provided by the father John Jay, and reinforced by William's own religious convictions, to final commitment to abolitionism as a way of life, was not without internal conflict for William. But as antiabolitionist intransigency increased, as the opposition became more hostile and even violent, Jay identified more and more with the oppressed, increased his hostility toward the oppressor and moved to final commitment. He could write in 1843:

> My life is devoted to the slave . . . in obedience to the will of God, and if he is pleased with my course, the opinion of others is of little moment . . . . I am also preparing for an assault on the proslavery abominations of my own church.[73]

Theodore S. Wright

Theodore S. Wright, the first black graduate of a theological seminary in the United States, was born in Providence, Rhode Island, in April 1797 to free parents.[74]

His father, R. P. G. Wright, for many years a resident of Schenectady, New York, was a delegate to the 1817 convention of free black Americans held in Philadelphia to protest the recently organized American Colonization Society.[75] This

[71] Tuckerman, *William Jay*, p. 118.

[72] Jay to Gerrit Smith, 8 September 1843, GSMC.

[73] Ibid.

[74] Carter G. Woodson, ed., *Negro Orators and Their Orations* (Washington, D.C.: Associated Publishers, 1925), p. 81.

[75] Bella Gross, "Life and Times of Theodore S. Wright, 1797–1847," *Negro History Bulletin* 3 (June 1940): 133.

convention, which the elder Wright helped organize, was attended by over three thousand blacks who denounced the policies of expatriation as "little more merciful than death,"[76] and it became the nucleus of the National Negro Convention Movement which Theodore S. Wright later helped to develop.

A contemporary of Theodore's father, the prominent black physician, James McCune Smith, described him as one of the most progressive men, who, from the earliest period of the antislavery struggle, advocated direct action. R. P. G. Wright was also one of the few black leaders who, from the start, advocated the higher education of Negro youth.[77]

The resonance to abolitionism induced by the model provided by the father was reinforced for Theodore when he attended the Free African School of New York City. Here under the tutelage of Samuel E. Cornish,[78] pastor of the First Colored Presbyterian Church, Theodore learned the tactics of the antislavery struggle as well as the basic curriculum. "Cornish had a great influence over him and later the two became co-workers and collaborators."[79]

Between 1825 and 1828 Wright attended Princeton where he frequently described the "evils of colonization" to students at the college.[80] In 1827 Samuel Cornish began issuing *Freedom's Journal*, an anticolonization newspaper, to which students at Princeton, including Wright, subscribed.[81] The president of the college, Dr. Miller, presented Wright with a situation of hostile opposition as he "forbade the students and teachers to get or read *Freedom's Journal*."[82] Miller

---

76 Ibid., p. 136.
77 Ibid., p. 133.
78 See p. 92.
79 Gross, "Life and Times," p. 134.
80 Woodson, *Negro Orators*, p. 85.
81 Charles H. Wesley, "The Negroes of New York in the Emancipation Movement," *Journal of Negro History* 24 (January 1939): 71.
82 Gross, "Life and Times," p. 134.

published open letters denouncing Wright's mentor and friend, Cornish, and the subscribers to the periodical as enemies of America and poisoners of the minds of Negro youth.[83] He threatened to dismiss anyone who dared challenge his views.

In 1828 upon his graduation from Princeton, Wright was called to the First Colored Presbyterian Church in New York City to succeed Samuel Cornish.[84] He was officially ordained by the Albany presbytery in 1829.[85] The church became the "university" for many black youths excluded by poverty and prejudice from the American educational system.[86]

Wright helped to organize many literary and antislavery societies in which he figured prominently for years. In 1833 he was vice president of the Phoenix Society in New York City whose main object was "to promote the improvement of the coloured people in morals, literature and the mechanical arts." Black and white abolitionists made regular visits to the homes of Negroes who were encouraged to organize educational and social bodies and to send their children to school.[87]

Wright used his position as minister in the thirties and throughout his life to further the work to which he committed himself—the liberation of the Negro people. Despite opposition from many colleagues and abolitionists Wright maintained his connection with the national presbytery in order to combat anti-Negro and proslavery feelings that dominated the majority of organizations affiliated with it. Wright preferred to challenge the church from within and thus unlike many other abolitionists refused to leave it.[88]

[83] Ibid.
[84] Wesley, "Negroes of New York," p. 82.
[85] *Colored American*, 3 June 1837.
[86] Gross, "Life and Times," p. 133.
[87] *Minutes and Proceedings of the Third Annual Convention for Improvement of Free People of Color* (Philadelphia, 1833), pp. 38ff.
[88] Gross, "Life and Times," p. 135.

In 1837 Theodore Wright became a leader in the United
Anti-Slavery Society of New York City which aimed to co-
ordinate the work of various Negro organizations. He was
also active at this time on the New York Vigilance Committee,
of which David Ruggles was secretary.[89] He was on the executive committees of several abolitionist groups and was in great
demand as a speaker.

When the schism in antislavery ranks came in 1840, Wright
stood firmly in his support of political action, but tried to
keep all the Negro groups united on the common grounds
of abolition and the "practical needs of the colored people."
Wright never allowed the abolitionists to forget the immediate
needs of free blacks who were "free only in name."[90] He challenged the antislavery societies just as he challenged the
religious organizations to "annihilate in their own bosoms
the cord of caste." The doctrine of many abolitionists, Wright
charged, "is to set the slave free and let him take care of
himself."[91] He insisted that "prejudice must be killed or
slavery will never be abolished."[92]

Theodore S. Wright, a highly educated black American,

[89] David Ruggles (1810–1849), born of free parents, was one of New
York State's top one hundred abolitionist leaders. He was a grocer in
New York City from 1829–1833, when he gave up the business to become an agent for the *Emancipator*. He published three issues of the
Mirror of Liberty, 1838–1839, but his mark was made with the Vigilance
Committee which was organized to see that alleged fugitive slaves received
due process, and to prevent the kidnapping of free blacks in the city
and their sale to the South as slaves. Between 1835 and 1837 the committee, with Ruggles as secretary, claimed to protect 335 persons (*Report
of the New York State Vigilance Committee* [New York, 1853], p. 2).

By 1841 David Ruggles was a relatively militant black man who called
for fellow blacks, free and bound, to "Rise, brethren, rise! Strike for
freedom, or die slaves" (*Liberator*, 13 August 1841).

[90] *Colored American*, 30 May 1840; Gross, "Life and Times," p. 137.

[91] *Address Made Before the New York State Anti-Slavery Society's
Convention Held at Utica, September 20, 1837*. This speech is reprinted
in Woodson, *Negro Orators*, pp. 86–92.

[92] Ibid.

came to identify with oppressed Negroes. His attraction to abolitionism was likely induced by the model provided by his father who early was active in the antislavery crusade, and was intensified by his relationship with abolitionist Samuel Cornish. His commitment probably increased during his religious training and undeniably each time he, as a black man, confronted the "ever-present, ever-crushing Negro-hate,"[93] a phenomenon which was pervasive in the North especially in cities such as New York.

Samuel Ringgold Ward

Samuel R. Ward, of whom Frederick Douglass said, "In depth of thought, fluency of speech, readiness of wit, logical exactness and general intelligence, [he] has no successor in the race,"[94] was born on a plantation on the eastern shore of Maryland to slave parents in 1817. The family escaped to Greenwich, New Jersey, in 1820, and removed six years later to New York City.[95]

In New York, Ward's father was a house painter, whose experience under slavery seems to have induced in the son a resonance to abolitionism. Samuel Ward wrote "among the heaviest of my maledictions against slavery is that which it deserves for keeping my poor father—and millions like him—in the midnight and dungeon of the grossest ignorance."[96]

Poverty compelled Samuel to work, "but inclination led

93 For more on "Negro-hate" see p. 86.

94 Frederick Douglass, *Life and Times of Frederick Douglass* (New York: Pathway Press, 1941), p. 345.

95 Fred Landon, "Samuel Ringgold Ward," *Dictionary of American Biography*, ed. by Allen Johnson, vol. 19 (New York: Charles Scribner's Sons, 1936), p. 440.

96 Samuel R. Ward, *Autobiography of a Fugitive Negro* (London: Snow Publishers, 1855), p. 6.

[him] to study." He was placed in a public school and taught "by Mr. Adams, a Quaker gentleman."[97] He seems also to have attended Oneida Institute for a time. Thus, in spite of poverty, Ward was able to make some progress in learning.

Poverty, however, was not the only obstacle for a black lad in New York City. There was also "the ever-present, ever-crushing Negro-hate." The phenomenon of Negro-hate and its effect on Ward described below may easily have increased Ward's identification with the oppressed, his hostility toward the oppressor, and intensified his commitment to movements based on serving fellow blacks:

Negro hate . . . hedges up [the black person's] path, discourages his efforts, damps his ardour, blasts his hopes, and embitters his spirits.

Some white persons wonder at and condemn the tone in which some of us blacks speak of our oppressors . . . they [should] wonder rather that, what with slavery and Negro-hate, the mass of us are not either depressed into idiocy or excited into demons. This peculiarly American spirit . . . was ever at my elbow. As a servant it denied me a seat at the table with my white fellow servants; in the sports of childhood and youth, it was ever disparagingly reminding me of my colour and origin; along the streets it ever pursued, ever ridiculed, ever abused me. If I sought redress, the very complexion I wore was pointed out as the best reason for my seeking it in vain; if I desired to turn to account a little learning, in the way of earning a living by it, the idea of employing a black clerk was preposterous—too absurd to be seriously entertained. I never knew but one coloured clerk in a mercantile house . . . but he never was advanced a single grade. . . . So if I sought a trade, white apprentices would leave. If I were admitted; and when I went to the house of God, as it was called, I found all the Negro-hating usages and sentiments of general society there encouraged and embodied in the Negro pew, and in the disallowing Negroes

[97] Ibid., p. 7.

to commune until *all the whites,* however poor, low and degraded, had done. I know of more than one coloured person driven to the total denial of all religion, by the religious barbarism of white New Yorkers and other Northern champions of the slaveholder.[98]

Ward worked for a time as a clerk in David Ruggles's[99] grocery store where he may have been imbued with some of Ruggles's militancy, and in 1833 "it pleased God to answer the prayers of [his] parents, in [his] conversion."[100] It was in 1833 as well that the New York Anti-Slavery Society was established in New York City. Ward did not commit himself early, however. "Having been abused, and befooled, and slandered, disparaged, ridiculed, and traduced by the Colonizationists, we could not," he wrote, "but look on, first with very great distrust any persons stepping forward with schemes professedly for our own good."[101]

Samuel taught for a time in a school for black children, and in 1839 he was licensed to preach by the New York Congregational Association assembled at Poughkeepsie.[102] He was, in 1841, pastor of the Congregational Church of South Butler, New York. The congregation were all white persons save Ward's own family. He resigned this pastorate in 1843 because of throat trouble which was cured some months later. And in 1846 he was pastor of the Congregational Church in Cortland Village, New York.

In 1839 Ward had also taken a position as traveling agent of the American and New York State Anti-Slavery Societies; and between 1840 and 1850 he "preached or lectured in every church, hall, or schoolhouse in western and central New

---

98 Ibid., pp. 28–30.
99 See p. 84.
100 Ward, *Autobiography,* p. 30.
101 Ibid., p. 44.
102 Landon, "Samuel Ringgold Ward," p. 440.

York."[103] While Ward made his case for antislavery from a
Christian perspective, denouncing the buying and selling of
members of Christ's body, and denouncing the "adultery,
fornication, incest" with which slavery was associated, and
simply declaring the institution sinful,[104] he was more of a
platform orator than a preacher. "His aim seemed to be not
so much to preach the gospel of heaven as to preach the gospel
of this world that men calling themselves Christians might
learn to respect the natural and political rights of their fel-
lows."[105]

Ward seriously believed that the prejudice of whites against
blacks "is a constant source of temptation to the latter to hate
the former" but prayed that his people would be saved from
that hatred. While Ward asked his people to be forgiving, he
refused to countenance submissiveness and encouraged what
might be known in the modern day as black power. The
multiplicity of wrongs inflicted on the Negro, Samuel Ward
argued, made frequent black meetings and independent black
organizations indispensable. White people would appreciate
this need, he thought, if they had "worn a colored skin from
October 1817 to June 1840, as I have, in this pseudo-republic."
Ward was especially contemptuous of the "abolitionists in
profession" who had yet to conquer prejudice within themselves, and who "best loved the colored man at a distance."[106]

Ward's knowledge, through his father, of the disabling effect
of slavery, his own experience, as a black person, with the
phenomenon of Negro-hate and the milder but no less effective
prejudice of "liberals," in combination with his religious
convictions and training, made it highly likely that this fugitive would commit himself to abolitionism.

[103] Woodson, *Negro Orators*, p. 193.
[104] Ward, *Autobiography*, p. 68.
[105] Woodson, *Negro Orators*, p. 193.
[106] *National Anti-Slavery Standard*, 2 July 1840.

Henry Highland Garnet

Henry Highland Garnet was born into slavery in New Market, Maryland, on 23 December 1815.[107] In 1824, his parents, after receiving permission to leave the plantation to attend a funeral, escaped with him to Pennsylvania and moved to New York City in 1826. Thus Henry not only knew slavery from nine years of personal experience, but learned also the difficulties surrounding flight from oppression.

Between 1826 and 1828, Garnet was educated at African Free Schools of the city. In 1829 he took a job as a cook on a schooner which plied between New York City and Washington, D.C.[108] On returning from one of these trips in 1829, Henry discovered that slave catchers had invaded the Garnet home. His mother and father barely escaped; his sister was tried as a fugitive from labor.[109] Henry Garnet's immediate reaction to the mistreatments of his family was to purchase a knife and walk up Broadway in the hope that the slave catchers would try again.[110] The long-range result, however, was the intensification of Henry's identification with the oppressed, and an increase in resonance to antislavery.

Poverty apparently forced Garnet to indenture himself between 1829 and 1830. During his service one of his legs was injured permanently, becoming a constant physical reminder to Henry of black dependency.[111]

[107] "Henry Highland Garnet," *Appleton's Cyclopedia,* ed. by J. G. Wilson and John Fiske, vol. 2 (New York: D. Appleton and Co., 1888), p. 601.

[108] Carter G. Woodson, "Henry Highland Garnet," *Dictionary of American Biography,* ed. by Allen Johnson, vol. 7 (New York: Charles Scribner's Sons, 1931), p. 154.

[109] W. M. Brewer, "Henry Highland Garnet," *Journal of Negro History* 13 (January 1928): 39.

[110] Ibid.

[111] Ibid., p. 40.

In 1831 Garnet continued his studies in the High School for Colored Youth in New York. When Henry reached eighteen years of age, he joined the Sunday school of the First Colored Presbyterian Church and was baptized by Theodore S. Wright, "who became his patron and friend; looked upon him as his own son in the gospel."[112] Between 1833 and 1835 Wright, who saw Garnet's possibilities for training for the ministry and the cause of abolition, educated Garnet and guided him to what would eventually be prominent leadership in the Negro liberation movement.[113] Wright's mantle was passed to H. H. Garnet just as Samuel E. Cornish had passed his on to Wright.

In 1835 Garnet went to Canaan Academy, New Hampshire. Henry did not escape "Negro-hate" in this rural community. A mob using ninety-five oxen and working two days pulled the building which housed the academy out of line of the other buildings and burned it to the ground. "The mob further attacked Garnet in the home of Mr. Kimball with whom Garnet was boarding."[114]

Henry Garnet removed from this hostile atmosphere to the Oneida Institute to continue his education. Here he came under the tutelage of abolitionist Beriah Green. Henry graduated with honors in 1840, and removed to Troy the same year, where he taught in a colored school while studying theology under Dr. Nathaniel Beman, leading New School clergyman.[115] Garnet was licensed to preach in 1842 and remained in Troy nearly ten years as pastor of Presbyterian churches. He divided his time between preaching and agitation in the antislavery cause.[116]

[112] Alexander Crummel, *Africa and America* (Springfield: Wiley and Co., 1891), p. 277.
[113] Gross, "Life and Times," p. 135.
[114] Brewer, "Henry Highland Garnet," p. 41.
[115] "Henry Highland Garnet," p. 601.
[116] Brewer, "Henry Highland Garnet," p. 43ff.

Garnet was one of the most radical abolitionist leaders in New York State. This fact is easier to understand when one keeps in mind not only that he was carefully taught by Theodore S. Wright and Beriah Green, but also the negative events in this black man's life which led him along the road to commitment. "Slaves who had themselves felt the lash [or saw people close to them undergo this punishment] were skeptical of mere moral suasion as a means of converting America, slaveholders included, to an antislavery viewpoint."[117] Thus Garnet early opted for political action and was "the first colored man that ever attached his name" to the Liberty party.[118]

Moreover, given the fact that Garnet's experience not only included nine years of slavery, and the frightful experience of flight from bondage, but also mistreatment of his family by whites and mob violence against himself, he was not convinced of the efficacy of mere political action. By 1843 Henry Highland Garnet was committed to the cause of abolitionism enough to declare, "Brethren, arise, arise! strike for your lives and liberties. Now is the day and hour . . . you cannot be more oppressed than you have been—you cannot suffer greater cruelties than you have already. Rather die freemen than live to be slaves. Remember that you are four millions;"[119] and "It is an old and true saying that 'if hereditary bondmen would be free, they must themselves strike the blow.' "[120]

Garnet's views were not supported by a majority of those

117 Herbert Aptheker, "The Negro in the Abolitionist Movement," *Science and Society* 5 (1941): 17.

118 H. H. Garnet to Mrs. Maria W. Chapman, 11 November 1843, cited in Carter G. Woodson, *Mind of the Negro as Reflected in Letters Written During the Crisis, 1800–1860* (Washington, D.C.: Associated Publishers, 1920), p. 194.

119 Quoted in Woodson, *Negro Orators*, p. 154.

120 Quoted in H. H. Garnet, *A Memorial Discourse (1865)*, with introduction by J. M. Smith, "Sketch of the Life and Labors of Rev. Henry Highland Garnet," (Philadelphia: J. M. Wilson, 1865), p. 47.

voting at the National Convention of Colored Citizens held in Buffalo in 1843.[121] But it is probably safe to say that this same majority did not experience the kind and amount of punishment and suffering Garnet had undergone at the hands of white oppressors.

Samuel E. Cornish and Charles B. Ray

Samuel E. Cornish was born in Sussex County, Delaware, in 1795. In 1815 he moved to Philadelphia where he was educated in the Free African Schools and became a candidate for the ministry in the Presbyterian church.[122]

He came to New York City in 1821 and organized the First Colored Presbyterian Church in January 1822 and continued as its pastor until 1827 when he was succeeded by Theodore S. Wright.[123]

In 1827 Cornish was an agent for the Free African Schools and for the Phoenix Society, and he worked for the establishment of a Negro Manual Labor College. None of these activities provided much opportunity for agitation, but all aimed at solving effectively the problems of black Americans. In the same year he issued *Freedom's Journal*, a periodical with the primary aim of exposing colonization as inappropriate to the needs of free Negroes and black slaves. In an early issue Cornish wrote: "I do not believe that our Southern brethren in general intend to do anything more than to provide a sort of safety valve by this society to serve as an outlet for their free blacks and supernumeraries."[124]

[121] *Minutes of the National Convention of Colored Citizens* (Buffalo, New York, August 1843), p. 13.

[122] H. N. Christian, "Samuel Cornish, Pioneer Negro Journalist," (Master's thesis, Howard University, 1936), p. 3.

[123] Wesley, "The Negroes of New York," p. 82.

[124] *Freedom's Journal*, 30 March 1837. See also Samuel E. Cornish, *The Colonization Scheme Considered* (Newark: A. Guest, 1840).

After publishing *Freedom's Journal* for two years, Cornish established a newspaper, *Rights of All*, to fight not only colonization but prejudice. In 1834 he was elected to the board of managers of the American Anti-Slavery Society, and in 1837 in addition to holding an executive position with the Committee of Vigilance, he edited the *Colored American* dedicated to "emancipation without expatriation—the extirpation of prejudice—the enactment of equal laws and a full and free investiture of [Negroes'] rights as men and citizens."[125]

Samuel E. Cornish, with religious sensibilities aroused through training for the ministry, was a black man who spent most of his adult life in New York. The city was marked by an "ever-present, ever-crushing Negro-hate" which undoubtedly helped Cornish to decide to commit himself to abolitionism and the cause of free blacks.

Charles Ray was born on 25 December 1807 in Falmouth, Massachusetts, where his father was a mail carrier. Charles was educated at schools and academies of his native town.[126] Afterwards he worked for five years on his grandfather's farm in Westerly, Rhode Island.

In the early 1830s, Ray, financed by the abolitionists, studied at Wesleyan Seminary in Wilbraham, Massachusetts, and Wesleyan University in Middletown, Connecticut. Southern and northern white students raised objections to his presence at the university, calling it "inexpedient." Charles was forced to leave.[127]

In 1832 he opened a boot and shoe store in New York City and in the following year joined the American Anti-Slavery Society. Financed by Lewis Tappan, Ray was also very active

[125] *Colored American*, 11 March 1837.
[126] Harold G. Villard, "Charles B. Ray," *Dictionary of American Biography*, ed. by Allen Johnson, vol. 15 (New York: Charles Scribner's Sons, 1935), p. 403.
[127] *Liberator*, 12 January 1833.

in working the underground railroad.[128] In 1834 Ray was ordained a Methodist minister. He was a pastor for more than thirty years, which included a twenty-two year tenure with the Bethesda Congregational Church.

Charles B. Ray, having experienced at least once the hostility of whites who inflicted suffering on him, became an abolitionist who directly aided fugitive slaves, an editor who crusaded for black liberation, a member of the New York African Society for Mutual Relief, and a trustee of a corporation to aid black education.[129] He was obviously busy promoting a literal attainment of his objectives.

Ray had no "disposition to sit idly by when there is so much Christian work within reach and pressing upon one's hands to do." Christian work was rest for him—"to look and not to do is not rest."[130]

James Caleb Jackson

James C. Jackson was born in Manlius, Onondaga County, New York, 28 March 1811. His father was a physician, but because of poor health he gave up his practice and retired to the farm when James was twelve.

In 1828 the future editor of several abolitionist journals entered Manlius Academy to prepare for college. However, the death of his father prevented the completion of academic

[128] The underground railroad was not, according to recent research, highly systematic nor extensive. See Larry Gara, *The Liberty Line* (Lexington: University of Kentucky Press, 1961); but such as it was, blacks ran it almost wholly by themselves up to 1835. See also Aptheker, "Negro in the Abolitionist Movement," pp. 2–23.

[129] Florence T. Ray, *Sketch of the Life of Reverend Charles B. Ray* (New York: J. J. Little and Co., 1887), p. 14.

[130] Ibid., p. 17.

work for James C. Jackson. And after marrying on 10 September 1830 he abandoned all plans for a college education.[131]

Jackson was early interested in religion and reform which in his view were intimately connected: "The subject of anti-slavery involving as it does great moral principles is calculated to aid much in the discussion of the preeminently great question of Christian Union—the right of Church fellowship its true basis—the right and manner of Church organization. I am persuaded that one of the greatest sins in the land is Sectarianism. . . . What is Slavery? It is the denial of Natural equality in respect to *Rights*. What is Sectarianism? It is the denial of the doctrine of Christian Equality."[132]

After seven years of antislavery activity, Jackson moved away from the nonresistance Garrisonians and into the camp of the political abolitionists. He was invited by Gerrit Smith to come to Peterboro, New York, and he settled there in 1838. In 1840 he was made secretary of the American Anti-Slavery Society, and over the next six years he was involved in editing the *National Anti-Slavery Standard, The Madison County Abolitionist, The Liberty Press,* and the *Albany Patriot.*[133]

Poor health forced Jackson to give up journalism. During the months of his illness he had been under the care of doctors, with whom he joined in a partnership in 1848, opening a hygienic institute known as the "Glen Haven Water Cure." In 1858 Jackson opened a water cure in Dansville, New York, that became famous as "Our Home Hygienic Institute." His interest in reform continued.[134]

It is possible that the son of a physician, having relatively high aspirations for himself which were frustrated by events

---

131 Frank Monaghan, "James Caleb Jackson," *Dictionary of American Biography,* ed. by Allen Johnson, vol. 9 (New York: Charles Scribner's Sons, 1932), p. 547.
132 Jackson to Gerrit Smith, 26 June 1838, GSMC.
133 Monaghan, "James Caleb Jackson," p. 547.
134 Ibid.

beyond his control, such as a father's death, might become "tension-ridden." Whether James C. Jackson joined the anti-slavery movement for the "action" in order to reduce this hypothetical tension, however, is impossible to tell with the scant amount of knowledge we have of him. Furthermore, his reform activity continued long and intensely after he attained status as a physician of note, at least equal to his father.

In any case, given Jackson's religious principles, it is just as possible that the motivation for his antislavery activity was reflected in the following letter to Gerrit Smith:

> I am in favor of a distinct political organization—for these reasons:
>
> . . . Respect for our principles demand it. . . . Respect for ourselves requires it. . . . 'Come out from among them and *be ye separate* and touch not the unclean thing and I will receive you.' *Jesus Christ*—[.][135]

The range of types of men involved in top and high-ranking abolitionist leadership is obviously wide. For a phenomenally wealthy Gerrit Smith there is a chronically impoverished Joshua Leavitt. Gerrit Smith inherited the bulk of his fortune; Lewis Tappan in contrast made his on his own. There were some abolitionists with higher status than their fathers such as Alvan Stewart, Beriah Green, and Samuel R. Ward, and others like James C. Jackson and William Jay who perhaps did not quite "measure up."

Included among the top and high-ranking abolitionists were a former slaveholder along with two fugitive slaves; a relatively uneducated free black and the first black graduate of Princeton Theological Seminary; a son of a Supreme Court Chief Justice holding an important judgeship himself for

[135] Jackson to Gerrit Smith, November 1838, GSMC.

twenty-five years, and a struggling journalist; a man who lost his father at fourteen, another who had a lifelong relationship with his father.

Most of the men detached themselves from their churches in order to criticize them from without, and at least one, Theodore S. Wright, decided to attempt change from within. Most thought political action would eventuate in relative success; Henry H. Garnet thought bloodshed necessary; James G. Birney was "temperamentally allergic to enthusiasm," others were not.

Despite this range of differences there are significant similarities that we might note at this point. Nine of these fifteen men had at least a college education, eleven were from urban areas, and four had legal training. Most important, of the fifteen top and high-ranking abolitionist leaders, all resided either in the "burned-over" district or in other areas which experienced major revivals between 1825 and 1835; all were intensely and actively religious. Five were ministers the better part of their adult lives, and seven had had theological training and served congregations at least part of their adult lives. Of the eight who had no theological training, five had significant conversion experiences in the years between 1826 and 1833. Henry B. Stanton, James G. Birney, Beriah Green, and Lewis Tappan were all directly influenced by Charles Grandison Finney, the great evangelist, or by Theodore Dwight Weld, Finney's foremost convert and collaborator in the work of salvation.

Highly educated, urban, intensely religious, constantly exposed to evangelicalism, eleven of the fifteen having theological or legal training, others having fathers or close relatives or older associates who were actively engaged in the work of salvation, these men resonated to abolitionism.

They did not become radicals overnight. After taking risks on behalf of the slave, eleven of these fifteen men were victims of violence, pain or suffering inflicted on them (in most cases more than once) by antiabolitionists. Three others were witness to violence inflicted by mobs on antislavery people and black people. Their experience with suffering increased their identification with the oppressed, their commitment to the cause of antislavery, and their willingness to take risks. This led to further suffering and further commitment until a "point of no return" was reached.

While I think this "composite" is significant, we do not have to rely on this relatively small sample. The next chapter will evolve a composite portrait based on information concerning one hundred abolitionist leaders.

4

Abolitionist Leadership: A Composite Portrait

To put the abolitionist leaders as political radicals in perspective, statistical information about them will be compared with relevant information on the core society and on a nonradical political leadership group in that society—congressmen representing districts in New York State from 1838 to 1845. Congressmen, while leaders, were not radical by any definition. Unlike the abolitionist leaders, congressmen as a group were not part of a social movement, nor were they committed—no less committed to ideas which were radical in substance, nor did they agitate.

A number of historians have followed the lead of David Donald[1] and maintained that abolitionist leaders were men whose fathers were high-status members of their respective com-

---

[1] David Donald, "Toward a Reconsideration of Abolitionists," *Lincoln Reconsidered* (New York: Alfred A. Knopf, 1956).

munities; but the sons were "elbowed aside" by the "merchant prince, the manufacturing tycoon, the corporation lawyer." The suggestion is that an economic revolution, transferring leadership from the countryside to the city, created a displaced and frustrated group in America, and that abolition provided an opportunity for agitation to relieve the frustration.

Yet the "burned-over district," that portion of New York State lying west of the Catskill and Adirondack Mountains, and where the majority of New York State's abolitionist leadership resided in the 1830s and 1840s had only reached "a stage of economy either of full or of closely approaching agrarian maturity."[2] This "dominantly rural water-power manufacturing economy which achieved maturity by 1837 was not before the Civil War seriously encroached upon by the advance agents of an urban industrial age."[3] The merchant prince, moreover, was not new to the 1830s; he had long been in the ascendency in the United States. Russel Nye writes that already by 1800 New England's "polity and society were controlled by a small number of sea traders, bankers, and merchants of wealth both inherited and new." The influentials of the Middle Atlantic states were likewise the shippers, bankers, and traders.[4] And along with the merchants, the professionals continued to hold high-prestige positions in antebellum American life. Richard Hofstadter cites Henry Adams's memory of New England as typical of the country at large:

Down to 1850 and even later, New England society was still directed by the professions. Lawyers, physicians, professors, mer-

2 Whitney Cross, *The Burned-Over District* (Ithaca: Cornell University Press, 1950), p. 76. Cross does not define the district in geographic terms as precisely as we would like. I have included those counties considered western and central which experienced evangelical revivalism and which have a place in Cross's study.

3 Ibid., p. 56.

4 Russel Nye, *The Cultural Life of the New Nation, 1776–1830* (New York: Harper and Row, 1960), p. 110.

chants were classes and acted not as individuals, but as though they were clergymen and each profession were a church.[5]

The thesis that such significant economic changes occurred in antebellum America as to effect a virtual revolution in status is at least questionable.

In any case if social dislocation and ensuing tensions were relevant to the creation of abolitionist leadership, then the class and status experience of abolitionist leaders should have differed in some fundamentally negative way from those of the nonabolitionist. Did it?

In 1850 in New York State, 888,294 males were in the labor force;[6] manufacturing tycoons and merchant princes in the broadest sense of the terms[7] made up slightly more than 6 percent of New York's male workers. Whether or not this 6 percent could elbow aside that part of New York's labor force consisting of doctors, teachers, preachers, and farmers in an era when these groups still "called the tune,"[8] becomes an even more irrelevant question in the light of the fact that within the ranks of eighty abolitionist leaders whose occupation I could determine, there were thirteen, or slightly more than 16 percent, merchants and manufacturers—relatively more princes and tycoons than New York's general working population contained. If there were a status revolution which favored persons engaged in commerce, it would appear that abolitionist leaders were leading it. This fact remains true even in comparison with congressmen from New York State,

5 Richard Hofstadter, *The Age of Reform* (New York: Alfred A. Knopf, 1955), p. 136.

6 United States, *Census of 1850* (Washington: A. O. P. Nicholson, 1854).

7 This figure for merchants includes all people listed as merchants, commission merchants, dealers, sellers, storekeepers, grocers in the United States *Census of 1850;* for manufacturers, everyone listed as manufacturer or maker.

8 Hofstadter, *Age of Reform*, p. 136.

of whom only 13.8 percent were active in mercantile enterprise.

Merchants who were abolitionist leaders in New York State included the very wealthy Lewis and Arthur Tappan, William Green, Jr., and John Rankin, all of New York City. Moreover, the ranks of abolitionists in New York State included the wealthy philanthropist, Gerrit Smith, and three bank presidents, John B. Edwards,[9] Reuben Sleeper, and Chauncey P. Williams.[10] While the question of wealth is only incidental to the kind of status question historians have raised, it might be noted here that of thirty-six rural towns from which abolitionist leaders came, and for which the average value of dwellings could be calculated, sixteen or 44.4 percent of these leaders came from very prosperous or unusually prosperous towns, another 19.5 percent came from prosperous towns.[11] These and other specific as well as impressionistic pieces of

---

[9] See p. 29.

[10] Reuben Sleeper (b. 1798), president of the Genessee River Bank, of Quaker descent, had a common school education. At sixteen he was a clerk, at twenty-three a merchant, at thirty-seven a bank president, and president of the board of trustees of the Town of Conesus. His home was reputedly a station on the underground railroad (James H. Smith, *History of Livingston County*, [Syracuse: D. Mason and Co., 1881], pp. 322–323). C. P. Williams (1817–1894), president of the National Albany Exchange Bank, educated in the common and high schools of Connecticut, spent his early life on his father's farm. In addition to his interest in finance, he worked incessantly for free and improved public schools (Amasa J. Parker, *Landmarks of Albany County*, [Syracuse: D. Mason, 1897], p. 370).

[11] Rural towns were assigned to five categories based upon the average value of dwelling per family in 1855: unusually prosperous ($800 and over); very prosperous ($600–799); prosperous ($400–599); marginal ($300–399); and poor ($100–299). These data are not available before the New York State *Census of 1855;* however, descriptions of the relative prosperity of towns within a county in the 1830s and 1840s found in county histories generally corresponded with the results obtained by computing the average value of dwelling per family for 1855. This design, in the main, follows that used by Lee Benson to determine the economic classification of political units for his study, *The Concept of Jacksonian Democracy* (Princeton: Princeton University Press, 1961).

evidence make it appear that there was at least as high a percentage of well-to-do men in the ranks of abolitionist leadership as in the ranks of other more conservative political leadership, and as in the core society.[12]

In New York State in 1850, slightly less than 2 percent of working males followed the occupations of teacher, editor, doctor, lawyer and clergyman; 66 percent of the congressmen were engaged in these activities, while just over 61 percent of New York's abolitionist leadership pursued these same callings. Of eighty abolitionists whose occupations I could determine, there were twenty ministers, fifteen lawyers, seven editors, five teachers, and four doctors. Only 10 percent of the abolitionist leaders farmed for a living, at a time when 35.4 percent of New York's general working population were farmers.[13]

It may be, given the relatively huge percentage of lawyers and ministers in the leadership of abolitionism (43.8 percent compared to slightly less than 1 percent for the general working population), that legal and theological training induced a resonance to movements based on helping others, including abolitionism. Theological training is probably more important than legal training here. 57 percent of the congressmen were lawyers while only 15 percent of the abolitionists practiced at the bar. However, 25 percent of the abolitionist leaders were ministers while none of the congressmen were ministers—although one of the 123 who held office between 1838

12 Other wealthy abolitionist leaders among the top one hundred in New York included: James G. Birney (see p. 38); Isaac Phelps, "leading farmer of Aurora"; Spencer Kellogg, mayor of Utica, 1841, with heavy investments in railroads and steam manufactures. (Daniel Wager, *Our County and its People* [Boston: Boston Historical Co., 1896], pp. 318, 350); Charles O. Shepard, president of Attica and Allegheny Railroad (Harry Douglass, *Progress with a Past,* [Arcade, N.Y.: Arcade Sesquicentennial and Historical Society, 1967], p. 167); and Alvan Stewart (see p. 47). Many others are described as "eminently successful in his profession," having "commodious property," being "leading merchant of the place," etc.

13 United States, *Census of 1850.*

and 1845, and about whom occupational information was available, had studied theology for a year.

Occupation	No. of Abolitionists	%	% of Congressmen	% of Working Population (1850)
Minister	20	25.0	0	0.5
Lawyer	15	18.8	56.9	0.5
Merchant	12	15.0	13.8	0.4
Farmer	8	10.0	6.5	35.4
Editor	7	9.7	3.3	0.03
Educator	5	6.2	1.6	0.3
Doctor	4	5.0	4.0	0.6
Bank Officer	4	5.0	7.3	0.03
Base:	80		123	

In any case, in addition to pursuing the professional and most influential callings in their respective communities, abolitionist leaders prior to 1840 were politically successful as well. Thirty-one of seventy-two about whom I could find information in addition to place of birth and residence, held a political position at some time before 1840. And between 1817 and 1839, 5 percent of them were holding office annually. In their ranks there were some "professionals" long used to the rough and tumble of politics like Congressman Seth Gates, E. D. Culver, and Thomas C. Love, and others like Asa Warren and Isaac Phelps.[14] But in the main the abolitionist lead-

[14] Asa Warren, supervisor of Eden, 1824, member of the state legislature, 1838, was also elected clerk of the Congregational church in his area for forty-seven consecutive years. Isaac Phelps, member of the state legislature, 1817–1818, town superviser for many years, was also magistrate in the Court of Common Pleas. (H. P. Smith, *History of the City of Buffalo and Erie County*, vol. 1 [Syracuse: D. Mason and Co., 1884], pp. 183, 321, 344, 545, 588, 590).

ers who participated in politics prior to 1840 were men like Joel G. Downer, who engaged in mercantile and agricultural pursuits and filled "various offices by the favor of his fellow citizens,"[15] such as town supervisor or magistrate—significant and influential positions on the local level.

Of sixteen abolitionist leaders whose pre-1840 political affiliation I could determine fifteen were Whigs and only one was a Democrat. Of 125 congressmen representing New York during 1838–1845 whose political affiliation I could determine eighty were Democrats and forty-five were Whigs. This overwhelming majority of Whigs in positions of abolitionist leadership is explained, at least in part, when we remember that in the 1830s and 1840s the Whig "political philosophy postulated an activist, positive state," responsible for improving the moral as well as the material well-being of society and capable of wielding broad powers. The Democratic philosophy on the other hand postulated a negative, passive state.[16] It is highly possible that men leading an activist moral and political crusade such as abolitionism, had originally—prior to the crusade—resonated to the Whig philosophy because it postulated activism and moralism. In any case, the abolitionist leaders were almost invariably associated with the Whig party and were actively engaged in public service prior to 1840 while they pursued high-status professions.

The educational level of abolitionist leadership was also relatively high. Of forty-two abolitionist leaders whose educational level I could determine, thirty-three or 78.6 percent of them attended academies or high schools, while only 52.3 percent of the congressmen had attended, and only 12.8 percent of the academy and high school age group in the general population attended such institutions in 1840. Twenty-four

15 L. M. Hammond, *History of Madison County* (Syracuse: Truait, Smith, and Co., 1872), p. 367.
16 Benson, *Concept of Jacksonian Democracy*, p. 212.

or 57.1 percent of the abolitionists graduated from college, while only 35.6 percent of the congressmen had, and only 0.3 percent of the college-age population of New York attended college in 1840. Even if we assume that the fifty or so abolitionists about whom I could find no educational information went no further than common school, the abolitionist leaders in New York State were a highly educated group.[17]

Education	No. of Abolitionists	%	% of Congressmen	Statewide % (1840)
Academy and other	33	78.6	52.3	12.8
College and above	24	57.1	35.6	0.3
	Base: 42	126		

The abolitionist leaders were also urban; however, the social composition of the movement itself was distinctly rural. With few exceptions the most important antislavery towns, indicated by the percentage of votes given to the Liberty party, were small, moderately prosperous farming communities. In fact there appears to have been an inverse relationship between Liberty voting and "urbanity."[18] However, of ninety-

[17] The percentage who attended academies would change to 36 percent compared to 50.7 percent for congressmen and 12.8 percent for the core society's age group; the percentage for college graduates would fall to 26 percent compared to 42 percent for the congressmen and 0.3 percent for the age group in the general population.

[18] Only one city in New York State (Utica) gave the Liberty party as much as 5 percent of its total vote. In every other city it received less than the state average (3.1 percent) and in most far less. See Benson, *Concept of Jacksonian Democracy*, p. 209; Alice Henderson, "The History of the New York State Anti-Slavery Society" (Ph.D. diss., University of Michigan, 1963), appendix; and John Hendricks, "History of the Liberty Party in New York State" (Ph.D. diss., Fordham University, 1958), appendix. For social composition, see also Cross, *Burned-Over District*, p. 226.

one abolitionist leaders whose 1840–1850 residence I could determine forty-six lived in cities of 12,000 or more population.[19] Thus 50.5 percent of New York abolitionist leaders were from urban areas. At the same time (1845) only 29.8 percent of the state's congressmen and only 24.4 percent of New York's general population lived in cities of 12,000 or more inhabitants. And in 1850 only 10 percent, roughly, of the American population resided in cities of this size.[20] From this we can deduce that the abolitionist movement in New York tended to draw its leadership from urban areas rather than from rural communities.

Urban, highly educated, moderately prosperous, pursuing the most influential occupations in their communities, and actively engaged in public service, the abolitionist leaders can be reasonably viewed as among the secure and substantial citizens of their towns and counties—men who were not being elbowed aside or losing status.

That the abolitionists, prior to their outspoken commitment to the movement, were respected, high-status citizens, however, does not "prove" that they were not dislocated or abnormally frustrated through a process of what some sociologists have called *"relative* deprivation."[21] Perhaps the fathers of the abolitionist leaders were of even higher status and were even more influential than their sons; and the sons because of this experienced a sense of failure in not "measuring up," thereby becoming overly frustrated.

If we use David Donald's status hierarchy, i.e., merchants, manufacturers, and lawyers being at least one rung higher than doctors, teachers, preachers, and farmers—we find that

19 New York State *Census of 1855* indicates the following cities with 12,000 or more population: Albany, Brooklyn, Buffalo, New York, Oswego, Rochester, Salina, Syracuse, Troy, and Utica.

20 United States, *Census of 1850.*

21 See Robert K. Merton, *Social Theory and Social Structure* (Glencoe, Illinois: Free Press, 1957), pp. 225–280.

four of the thirty or 13.5 percent of the abolitionists whose fathers' occupations I could determine had lower status than their fathers had had, fourteen of thirty or 46.5 percent had the same status as their fathers and twelve or 40 percent had higher status than their fathers.[22]

More important, however, whether the fathers had not remained long enough in one place, or had not been important enough, or could simply not afford to pay for the space, they were generally missing from the pages of biographical dictionaries and of their respective counties' histories. The little information I do have about them was gleaned from the biographies of their sons. This is a relatively strong, if impressionistic, indication that the fathers had, at least, no more prestige, were no richer, and received no more deference than their abolitionist sons.

And if we use a status hierarchy which places small farmers, teachers, millers, tanners, clerks and journalists below doctors, lawyers, ordained ministers, merchants, bankers, manufacturers, and planters, we find that 53 percent of the abolitionists had the same status as their fathers, 40 percent had higher status and 7 percent had lower status than their fathers. At the same time 50 percent of the congressmen representing New

[22] Twelve fathers had been farmers; of the abolitionist sons of these fathers only three were farmers, three were merchants, two were lawyers, two were ordained ministers, one was a teacher, and another a bank president. Three fathers had been doctors; their sons—two lawyers and one journalist who eventually became a physician. Six fathers were merchants; two of their sons were merchants, two were ministers, one a lawyer, and another a professional philanthropist. Four fathers were lawyers—two of the sons were lawyers, one a farmer, another a minister. Three fathers who were minister, house painter, and mail carrier respectively had abolitionist sons who were ministers. Finally, one innkeeper had an abolitionist offspring who was a merchant, and one well-to-do planter had a son who was a lawyer.

Similarly in the congressional group five of forty or 12.5 percent had lower status than their fathers, twenty or 50 percent had the same, and fifteen or 37.5 percent had higher status than their fathers.

York from 1838 to 1845 had the same status as their fathers, 37.5 percent had higher and 12.5 percent had lower status than their male parents. Thus the radical abolitionist leaders were slightly more upwardly mobile than the nonradical congressmen.

Most important of all, however, is the fact that a sizeable majority of the abolitionist leaders in New York State were actively and intensely religious. Forty-nine of seventy-two about whom I could find more than place of birth and residence (or 68 percent) had either been ministers (twenty-two), trustees or founders of churches, deacons, elders, missionaries, superintendents of Sunday schools, or active in evangelical societies. Similar positions were held by only six or 4.6 percent of the congressmen. Certain specific and impressionistic evidence indicates that the religious zeal of the abolitionist leaders was engendered and reinforced during their respective stays in New England and the "burned-over district" of New York State.

Twenty-eight of fifty-eight abolitionist leaders or 48.1 percent whose nativity I could determine were born in New England; only 33 percent of the congressmen were born in New England and in 1850 only 6.7 percent of New Yorkers at large had been born in New England. Furthermore, twenty-

Nativity	No. of Abolitionists	%	% of Congressmen	% of General Population
New England	28	48.1	33.1	6.7
New York	22	38.0	59.0	69.5
Other U.S.	6	10.3	6.3	3.0
Foreign	2	3.4	1.6	21.0
	Base: 58		127	

four of the twenty-eight abolitionists born in New England were born, and at least for a short time raised, in Massachusetts, Connecticut, and Vermont—those states that led all others in the evangelical tradition.[23]

Approximately 65 percent of New York abolitionist leaders were Yankees—i.e., were born in New England or had direct ancestors who were born there. Historians of New York State tend to agree that in the 1840s approximately 63.5 percent of New York's general population were Yankees.[24] While it appears that the ethnic variable—Yankee—is not overly significant, the fact that 48.1 percent of New York's abolitionist leaders were *born* in New England indicates that they were more recently removed from that evangelical area.

Ethnicity	No. of Abolitionists	%	% of General Population
Yankee	33	66	63.5
Yorker	3	6	11.8
Penn–Jerseyite	5	10	4.0
Negro	7	14	1.7
Foreign	2	4	15.0
	Base: 50		1850

Moreover, 70 percent of New York State's abolitionist leadership lived in the "burned-over district" of western New York in the late 1820s and early 1830s while only 48.5 percent of the congressmen and only slightly under 50 percent of the

[23] Cross, *Burned-Over District*, pp. 4–13.
[24] David M. Ellis et al, *A Short History of New York State* (Ithaca: Cornell University Press, 1957); Dixon Ryan Fox, *Yankees and Yorkers* (New York: New York University Press, 1940); Benson, *Concept of Jacksonian Democracy*.

general population lived there during the evangelical revivals. An additional 19 percent of abolitionist leadership lived in cities which experienced major revivals during the same period; only 14.6 percent of the congressmen and slightly under 11 percent of the general population of the state lived in these cities. It was during the 1820s and early 1830s that a "mighty revival" led by Charles Grandison Finney had begun in western New York. At the turn of the decade this revival burst all bounds and spread across the nation, becoming, in Gilbert Barnes's opinion, "the greatest of all modern revivals."[25] But western New York remained more intensively engaged in revivalism than other portions of the northeast.[26]

According to Whitney Cross in *Burned-Over District* and Timothy Smith in *Revivalism and Social Reform,* Finney's dynamic impact upon New York and the country at large came primarily from the great revival campaigns of 1826 and the early 1830s.[27] The message generally imparted at these revivals was that salvation demands not merely faith and divine grace, but also good works. Barnes writes that to the rejoicing "brethren fresh from the ardor of revival, social ills seemed easily curable and dreams of reform were future realities."[28] And Cross writes that the religious ultraism engendered by the revivalism of the 1830s was "the precedent condition to all ensuing crusades."[29]

The reform movements provided an established set of immediate objectives whose progressive realization could be counted steps toward the millennium. Religious enthusiasts contemplated an

[25] Gilbert H. Barnes, *The Anti-Slavery Impulse* (New York: D. Appleton-Century Co., 1933), p. 16.
[26] Cross, *Burned-Over District,* p. 11.
[27] Ibid., p. 156; Timothy Smith, *Revivalism and Social Reform* (Nashville, Tenn.: Abingdon Press, 1957), p. 181.
[28] Barnes, *Anti-Slavery Impulse,* p. 16.
[29] Cross, *Burned-Over District,* p. 208.

all-powerful God who had long since appointed the judgment day and yet felt themselves pressed to assist Him in bringing it to pass.[30]

Although Finney and many of his co-workers in the task of conversion were more concerned with saving men's souls than specific reforms, slavery was almost always mentioned at revivals as a symbol of sin—as the extreme manifestation of what was wrong with America. Religious leaders of all persuasions cooperated to kindle the blaze of antislavery feeling, for an "uncompromising stand against slavery as a sin fitted alike the pattern of Methodist perfectionism, New School revivalism, and the ethical concerns of radical Quaker and Unitarian religion."[31]

Religious revivalists placed the burden of guilt for slavery's continued existence upon themselves and their audiences and built among them a "present obligation" and a personal or immediate responsibility for the sin of slavery. Emancipation became, then, not only an "objective matter of social or political expediency," but, just as important, a "subjective act of purification and a casting off of sin."[32] Reflecting this, Alvan Stewart wrote: "I never mean to cease serving that God before whom we must all shortly appear to render up an account of our stewardship here on earth."[33]

I cannot as yet "prove" that all of New York's abolitionist leaders, or even most of them, attended revival meetings or were affected by them in such a way as to reinforce their respective resonances to reform movements. But the fact that such a majority of these leaders were actively religious—at least 68 percent of them were either ministers, deacons, elders,

[30] Ibid., p. 201.
[31] Smith, *Revivalism and Social Reform,* p. 180.
[32] Davis, "Emergence of Immediatism," p. 212.
[33] Alvan Stewart to Uriel Stewart, 12 July 1830, Stewart Collection, New-York Historical Society, New York. N.Y.

or otherwise involved in evangelical activity—the fact that
48.1 percent were born in New England, 41 percent in areas
with a strong evangelical tradition—and the fact that 89 percent of them lived in areas affected by major revivals during
1826–1833, allows us to assume that they were part of the
religious reawakening of this era.

As such, the New York abolitionist leaders shared a sense of
personal responsibility for the continued existence of the concrete sin of slavery, and all of them could have declared with
William Goodell:

> I am ready not only to labor and suffer perplexity and want, but
> indeed to wear my life out in this cause, if I may be instrumental
> in saving my country. . . .
>
> I have fought a good fight, I have finished my course, I have
> kept the faith: henceforth there is laid up for me a crown of
> righteousness, which the Lord, the righteous judge, shall give me
> at that day. . . .[34]

Although these statements reflect a certain concern for self,
they indicate also that the abolitionist believed his own moral
and political demands relevant to the needs of the slave and
the nation.

Indeed, for the abolitionist leader genuine concern for the
slave, the free Negro, and the general welfare was at the cen-
ter of the antislavery movement. While relatively few New
York State abolitionist leaders encouraged slave revolts, as did
Henry Garnet and David Ruggles, the great majority, especially after 1835, did participate in aiding fugitives. Their
homes were reputed to be stations on the underground railroad. Tappan and Smith among others financed escapes; William L. Chaplain, another of New York's top one hundred

---

[34] Quoted in [Lavinia Goodell], *In Memoriam: William Goodell*
(Chicago: Gilbert & Winchell, 1879), pp. 1, 24.

abolitionist leaders "went into the South [with the encouragement of many other New York State abolitionists] to bring the
message to the slaves themselves that there were people anxious
to see them free and ready to help them escape."[35]

The literature of New York State's abolitionist societies is
abundant with evidence that New York State abolitionist
leaders were concerned with the rights and civil liberties of
the free Negro as well as with freedom for the slave. The
Liberty party directed as much of its effort to improving the
condition of the northern free Negro as it did to emancipation.

While the efforts of white abolitionists in the direction of
aiding the free black were often fitful and abortive, this was
probably due much more to a certain romantic naivete[36] and
to the dialectic of direct political involvement than to lack of
concern and commitment.[37]

William Goodell believed in 1837 that as long as New York
laws discriminated against Negroes, especially in regard to
suffrage, the belief of Negro inferiority would be reinforced.
This belief was one of the strongest supports, he thought, not
only of slavery but of social and economic discrimination.[38]
Samuel H. Cox agreed that "emancipation is too limited, too
narrow," and asked that blacks "be immediately admitted to
share with us the blessings of equal citizenship."[39] Largely
through Arthur Tappan's efforts, Negroes were admitted to
Oberlin College; Lewis Tappan fought for, among other
things, the elimination of the "negro pew"; Gerrit Smith
financed a variety of educational institutions designed to aid

[35] Aptheker, "The Negro in the Abolitionist Movement," *Science and Society* 5 (1941): 2–23.

[36] See John Thomas, "Antislavery and Utopia," in *Antislavery Vanguard* ed. by Martin Duberman (Princeton: Princeton University Press), pp. 240–269.

[37] See chapter 6.

[38] *Friend of Man*, 19 January 1837.

[39] *First Annual Report of the American Anti-Slavery Society* (New York: Dorr and Butterfield, 1834), p. 4.

free blacks in the North, and distributed approximately 140,-000 acres of land to Negroes in an attempt at economic uplift; Beriah Green wrote in 1841 that "It is wicked and sinful to make a distinction because of color in any of the social relations of life . . . ;"[40] and Alvan Stewart in a letter to Samuel Webb gives us an indication of how inseparable abolitionism and the cause of the free black actually were in the minds of these leaders:

> The Anti-Slavery cause is as precious as ever and moves on with all the majesty of truth. I hope our state Convention in June next to amend the Constitution will make our colored people voters on the same terms as others. A great struggle this.[41]

All of this indicates that the discontent of abolitionist leadership was not essentially relieved nor guilt essentially discharged "in the very process of agitating," but that the leaders were sincerely concerned with a literal attainment of their objective.

Abolitionist leaders in New York State experienced a reawakened religious impulse.[42] This impulse, taken together with the strong sense of social justice it aroused when placed in the context of the phenomenally optimistic era of the 1830s and 1840s, appears to have been a powerful motivation for most social reformers as well as abolitionists.[43]

[40] *Onondaga Standard*, 27 January 1841.

[41] Alvan Stewart to Samuel Webb, 14 January 1846, Alvan Stewart Papers, New York State Historical Society, Cooperstown.

[42] This impulse should not be confused with institutional support by churches. Antislavery clergy were unable to convert their churches to their views and as a result were forced to leave their churches. On this point see Lorman Ratner, "Northern Opposition to the Anti-Slavery Crusade, 1830–40" (Ph.D. diss., Cornell University, 1960); Ralph Harlow, "Gerrit Smith and the Free Church Movement"; and Charles C. Cole, *Social Ideas of Northern Evangelists* (New York: Columbia University Press, 1954).

[43] Cross, *Burned-Over District*, p. 197; Filler, *Crusade Against Slavery* (New York: Harper & Bros., 1960), pp. 28ff.

The optimism of the era was both Christian and secular. It was in part the result of a theological revolution which unleashed egalitarian forces; for with the New School's emphasis on human ability, perfectionism—the belief in the ultimate perfectibility of man and society—became a key doctrine. The belief was reinforced by the increasing number and magnitude of revivals.

Moreover, the idea of political, social, and economic equality —or simply secular egalitarianism—which was vigorously rising during the transportation and communication revolution in the 1820s in New York State and elsewhere[44] contained "a supreme optimism, a belief in ultimate perfection of society through progressive improvement in humankind."[45] This secular optimism was stimulated further by gains in the acquisition of raw materials and markets, rapid increase of population, expansion westward to the Pacific and the subsequent uncovering of areas rich in natural resources; and many abolitionist leaders, affected by both the secular and religious stimuli to optimism, were convinced "that the progressive tendencies of the age were opposed to the continuance of slavery."[46] The "peculiar institution" would have no place in a perfected society.

For the moral reformer, perfection might come through a number of avenues. It might come simply when men avoided evil and consulted only conscience as a guide, or it might come when men joined with the like-minded and looked outward for perfect fellowship. Perfectionism thus in the first instance contained an anarchic appeal, and in the second a collectivist

[44] On this see Benson, *Concept of Jacksonian Democracy*, and George Rogers Taylor, *Transportation Revolution* (New York: Holt, Rinehart and Winston, 1964).

[45] Cross, *Burned-Over District*, p. 199.

[46] Arthur Ekirch, *The Idea of Progress in America, 1815–1860* (New York: Columbia University Press, 1944), p. 243.

call.[47] Most abolitionists probably felt attracted to both. The nonresistance Garrisonians, however, emphasized "a kind of glorious anarchy—organized without 'priests and rulers' ";[48] the political abolitionists, on the other hand, while they "believed progress to be attainable by human effort and practically inevitable," also derived "from their Calvinist traditions an equally powerful suspicion that the natural tendency, *unaided by willful diligence,* was toward degeneracy."[49] Translated into nonreligious terms this suspicion corresponds to the belief that individual action must fail to produce the desired results where collective action would succeed.[50] Furthermore, the political abolitionists generally believed that when Americans stopped "exempting Civil Government from the obligations of the Divine principles" success would come in all areas.[51] Thus in the minds of many political abolitionists were united the secular and religious stimuli to optimism.

The optimism of the abolitionist leader, moreover, was particularly reinforced when slavery was abolished in the British colonies between 1831 and 1833. In those years "a new generation of American reformers adopted the principle of immediatism, which had recently acquired the sanction of eminent British philanthropists."[52] The example "appealed with thrilling force"[53] and was a precedent which provided the abolitionists, according to Gilbert Barnes, with the most "immediate urge." Most of the abolitionist leaders in New York asked,

---

47 Thomas, "Antislavery and Utopia," p. 247.

48 John Demos, "The Anti-Slavery Movement and the Problem of Violent Means," *New England Quarterly* 37 (December 1964): 513.

49 Cross, *Burned-Over District,* p. 199. (Italics added.)

50 That the leaders of political abolitionism in New York State almost invariably had Whig histories lends support to this idea; Whigs tended toward collectivism, Democrats toward individualism.

51 Letter, Gerrit Smith to E. C. Delevan, 16 April 1852, GSMC,

52 Davis, "Emergence of Immediatism," p. 227.

53 Barnes, *Antislavery Impulse,* p. 102.

along with LaRoy Sunderland, why Americans should be "so far behind our brethren in England, in relation to this thing."[54]

British emancipation reinforced the faith of New York's abolitionist leadership that their demands would not go unheeded, that their agitation would not be in vain, that they would, after all, "substantially affect" the social order, and attain their objective of social justice.

[54] Quoted in Thomas Harwood, "British Evangelical Abolitionism and American Churches in the 1830's," *Journal of Southern History* 28 (August 1962): 292.

Reverend LaRoy Sunderland (1804–1885), one of the top one hundred abolitionist leaders in New York, organized the first antislavery organization in the Methodist church. In six consecutive sessions of the New England Conference, presiding officers from New York brought charges against him, ranging from slander to immorality.

5

Conclusion

ABOLITIONISM tended to draw its leadership from urban areas and from the highly educated, moderately prosperous segments of society. The abolitionist leaders pursued the most influential occupations in their communities and were actively engaged in public service. They generally seem to have had higher status in their respective communities than their fathers had had in theirs. It was impossible to find more than three or four men whose economic, social, or personal dislocation might reasonably be said to have left them discernably insecure and frustrated.

The New York abolitionist leaders were intensely and actively religious. They had been exposed to the revivalism of the era—a revivalism which was the "precedent condition to all ensuing crusades."[1] They were motivated by a reawakened religious impulse, a strong sense of social justice, and the sincere belief that they were not only insuring their own freedom from guilt, but that they would affect society in such a way as to assure social justice for everyone.

[1] Whitney Cross, *The Burned-Over District* (Ithaca: Cornell University Press, 1950), p. 208.

The leaders were concerned with the rights and civil liberties of the free Negro, and were concerned with the slave as a person as well as an abstract cause. There was a consistent pattern of violence, pain, and suffering inflicted upon the abolitionists after they took their respective first risks on behalf of the slave. This had the consequence, generally, of increasing the abolitionists' identification with the oppressed, and their resonance to abolitionism. The cycle usually continued until each was fully committed to the antislavery cause.

The abolitionists' intense religiosity, more than their psychological makeup, explains why they employed the terminology of sin and guilt. And their forcefulness in this area was a function of the frustration they suffered watching churches, parties, and ordinary citizens ignoring their pleas. That there was desperation in their appeals is explained by the fact that the abolitionists believed that America had become corrupted by its worship of the bitch-goddess success; that she was sacrificing the ideals of her own revolution and her Christian integrity on the altar of materialism; and that the nation thus had adopted a value hierarchy which placed private property, union, wealth, and future power above emancipation.

Yet too many historians have simply assumed that radical causes are primarily the manifestation of subjective feelings of frustration, principally produced by status dislocation. The leadership of abolitionism and, by implication, other radical leaders, can then, for these historians, only be frustrated people whose criticism and aggressiveness is based almost wholly on personal insecurity. Through this assumption, historians and other social scientists divest themselves of the necessity of debating the validity and merits of the radical's objectives.

The tension-reduction theory of radicals therefore has had wide appeal. The theory is found not only in David Donald's work, but also in the work of Stanley Elkins, who writes that "guilt may have been absorbed and discharged" during a reform movement "in ways which make unnecessary a literal attainment of the objective."[2] Avery Craven is influenced by the same theory when he writes about "maladjustments . . . complexes . . . repressed desires" and the "triumph of emotion over reason in the extremist's course."[3] Hofstadter, although less directly, implies the validity of the tension-reduction theory in his analysis of progressivism: the middle-class citizen suffered "through the changed pattern of deference and power." No longer calling the tune, "what he needed was a feeling that action was taking place."[4] And the critics of America's "radical right" believe that status dislocation and its ensuing frustrations are one of "the fundamental political forces operating in American Society."[5]

There has been, until recently, a widespread criticism of and alienation from the radical approach to change among professional intellectuals.[6] This alienation, according to sociologists like Kenneth Keniston, Erich Fromm, Nathan Glazer, and David Riesman, is symptomatic of automation; it is part and parcel of an increasingly technologized, specialized society.[7] One of the reasons for the "decline of enthusiasm and

[2] Stanley Elkins, *Slavery: A Problem in American Institutional and Intellectual Life* (Chicago: University of Chicago Press, 1959), p. 158.

[3] Avery Craven, *The Coming of the Civil War* (New York: Charles Scribner's Sons, 1942), p. 117.

[4] Richard Hofstadter, *The Age of Reform* (New York: Alfred A. Knopf, 1955), p. 138. Hofstadter, it should be noted, is not hostile to populism and progressivism; he assumes that both are strongly enough established in our tradition to withstand criticism. See also Hofstadter's essay "Wendell Phillips: The Patrician as Agitator," *American Political Tradition* (New York: Alfred A Knopf, 1948), p. 137.

[5] Seymour Lipset, "Sources of the 'Radical Right,'" in *New American Right,* ed. by Daniel Bell (New York: Criterion Books, 1955), p. 168.

[6] Kenneth Keniston, "Alienation and the Decline of Utopia," *American Scholar* 29 (1960): 162–163.

[7] Keniston, "Alienation and Decline of Utopia," p. 163; Erich Fromm, *The Sane Society* (New York: Holt, Rinehart, and Winston, 1960), passim; David Riesman and Nathan Glazer, "The Intellectuals and the Discon-

vitality among the liberal intellectuals in the last decade or
so," is that mass industrialized society has left the intellectual
with "a feeling of impotence and isolation."[8]

Keniston writes, however, that a more immediate reason
may very well have been "our unhappy experience with attempts to make real the visions of the past century—above all
the vision of Marx."[9] The failure of Marxism "undermined
our declining faith in our capacity to improve the world."[10]

The intellectual's rejection of enthusiasm and passion,
writes Arthur Mann, was reinforced in the 1940s and 1950s by

> a rising standard of living, increasing opportunities for scholars,
> cultural pluralism, the welfare state, and a healthy balance of
> power between big business, big labor, and big government.
> Living in such a going concern, few scholars acquired the kind
> of compassion, resentments, and hopes for a more egalitarian
> society that had enabled a previous generation to identify itself
> with economic and political reform.
>
> Instead, new perils to human welfare, like racism and totali-
> tarianism, directed attention to the dark sides of reform. . . . In
> such an atmosphere some liberals were ready to join disillusioned
> marxians in saying good-bye to ideology as they had known it.[11]

Whatever the reason or reasons for this widespread criticism
of radical change among intellectuals, whether it is a reaction
caused by the failure of Marxism, as Keniston suggests, or a
"recognition" of the darker side of reform brought on by the
events of the 1940s and 1950s, as Arthur Mann and C. Vann

---

tented Classes," in *New American Right,* ed. by Daniel Bell (New York:
Criterion Books, 1955), p. 80.

[8] Riesman and Glazer, "The Intellectuals and the Discontented Classes,"
p. 80.

[9] Keniston, "Alienation and Decline of Utopia," p. 183.

[10] Ibid.

[11] Arthur Mann, "The Progressive Tradition," in *The Reconstruction
of American History,* ed. by John Higham (New York: Hutchinson and
Co., 1962), p. 167.

Woodward write,[12] the criticism was indicative of a spreading "sense of political disengagement" among intellectuals.[13]

Psychoanalysis and social psychology had encouraged this disengagement to a certain extent.[14] For if it is believed that the political personality is merely displacing personal anxieties on the body politic, criticism of society ceases, suffocated by an atmosphere of intense suspicion of the critic. In our age, "crushing effects can be achieved by labeling one's adversaries as neurotic or psychopathic cases. It relieves one of the necessity of debating the merits of the adversaries' objectives."[15] In short, social protest can be explained away as a psychopathic symptom.

We cannot assume that historians are motivated to "explain away" social protest when they apply tension-reduction type theory, but this is often the logical implication of their arguments. A negative attitude toward social protest can lead to an anti-intellectual and unprofessional approach to analysis of change, especially in light of the fact that the psychological underpinnings of the tension-reduction theory of radicalism are either disproved, disputed, or ignored by modern psychologists. Moreover, a negative attitude toward social protest is dangerous to the health of our democracy, which is usually protected and maintained by "upheavals to shock the seats of power and privilege and furnish . . . periodic therapy."[16] For this tradition to endure, "the intellectual must not be alienated from the sources of the revolt."[17]

[12] Ibid; C. Vann Woodward, "The Populist Heritage and the Intellectual," *American Scholar* 29 (Winter 1959): 56–73.

[13] Philip Rieff, *Freud: The Mind of the Moralist* (New York: Doubleday, 1961), p. 266.

[14] Ibid., p. 267.

[15] Rudolf Heberle, *Social Movements* (New York: Appleton-Century-Crofts, 1951), p. 104.

[16] Woodward, "The Populist Heritage and the Intellectual," p. 72.

[17] Ibid.

6

An Impressionistic
Afterword

To draw the abolitionists as "normal" is not necessarily to imply that they were "right" either in ends or means. But at least if we are less prone to see these reformers as acting out their own psychic conflicts, we are in a better position to discuss the objective merits of their crusade.

Slavery was after all an anomaly. It was, to those whites who took both their Declaration of Independence and their Christianity seriously, a "peculiar institution," as even the South admitted. It was not only peculiar as a rigid, oppressive institution in a fluid, mobile, relatively unstructured American society, but was peculiar in most of the civilized world. In fact, except for Portugal and Spain, the "United States was the major deviant from standards of racial justice in the Atlantic Community."[1] It may be that those Americans who felt no guilt in the light of this were those furthest removed from reality.

[1] Bertram Wyatt-Brown, *Lewis Tappan and the Evangelical War Against Slavery* (Cleveland: Case Western Reserve University Press, 1969), p. xi.

Furthermore, had the abolitionists not stimulated public debate on slavery, there is a good possibility that no one else would have. And it was highly practical for the abolitionists to make their demands as intense and forceful as possible for it was necessary to undermine northern complacency and to shock into movement the intransigence of the South. The violence of the Civil War and Reconstruction, moreover, was more a result of southern overreaction to the not outrageous criticisms of slavery than of any activities of the radicals.

While many younger historians are in general agreement with this, there is still a good deal of dispute over the validity of the various tactics adopted by different wings of the abolitionist movement. The nonresistance, and antipolitical stances of William Lloyd Garrison and his followers, for example, have had until recently a relatively "bad press." The political abolitionists were thought the "realists" and thus more effective than the Garrisonians.

This view has been creditably challenged with the publication of Aileen Kraditor's *Means and Ends in American Abolitionism*.[2] Dr. Kraditor suggests that direct participation in politics by abolitionists diluted the moral appeal of their crusade, pushed them into compromises destructive of their highest ideals (most significantly racial equality) and inhibited the building of a constituency to support real freedom for blacks after emancipation. The motive of those abolitionists who entered the political arena, she writes, was to satisfy a desire to work within the mainstream of American life and to make abolitionism more respectable especially by divorcing it from Garrison) and thus more broadly attractive. Dr. Kraditor, then, sees the Garrisonians not only as more realistic than the Liberty men but more radical as well.

It is probably true that Garrison and some of his followers, in seeing so much of American life as corrupt, were more

[2] Aileen S. Kraditor, *Means and Ends in American Abolitionism* (New York: Pantheon, 1968).

radical than many of the Liberty party adherents who were willing to work within the "system." This view must, however, be qualified. For while it is tempting to assume that those who were willing to work inside the gates of the city saw less wrong with it, evidence indicates that for many of the high-ranking political abolitionists the elimination of slavery alone would not reinvigorate an otherwise good society. Many saw or came to see American society and its institutions as basically corrupt and in need of restructuring. This was certainly true, for example, of Gerrit Smith, Beriah Green and William Goodell.

Moreover, many political abolitionists shared Garrison's views on, and agreed with the aim of his pacifism, i.e., the creation of a truly Christian society, one based on love and thus a government less reliant on coercion. Gerrit Smith, James C. Jackson, Beriah Green, William Goodell, and even Lewis Tappan were close to the come-outerism of Garrison.[3] As George W. Julian, the antislavery congressman from Indiana, said, the political abolitionists were "theologically reconstructed through their unselfish devotion to humanity and the recreancy of the churches to which they had been attached. They were less orthodox, but more Christian."[4]

For these men the original Calvinist deity had died to be replaced by one concerned with the happiness of mankind and

---

[3] See Tappan's remarks in *The Minutes of the Christian Anti-Slavery Convention, Assembled April 17th–20th, 1850* (Cincinnati: 1850); William Goodell, *Come-Outerism: The Duty of Secession from a Corrupt Church* (New York: American Anti-Slavery Society, 1845). By 1844 Goodell was espousing a series of reforms designed to overhaul American society on the basis of "natural justice;" Smith ultimately refused to accept the Bible as the guide to religious truth (Ralph V. Harlow, "Gerrit Smith and the Free Church Movement," passim). Green's interpretation of Calvinism proved to be so radically different from that of surrounding clergy that all orthodox pulpits were closed to him.

[4] George W. Julian, *The Life of Joshua R. Giddings* (Indianapolis: Carlon & Hollenbeck, 1889), p. 401.

the establishment of a moral order which reflected the ethics but not the theology of Calvinism. On one level this could be seen as rather mainstream, reflecting the dynamic, optimistic faith of middle-class, nineteenth-century America. But when these abolitionists tried to put their faith into practice many of them experienced a severe frustration which impelled them to be more critical of the whole sweep of American life. Significant numbers were won over to a proto-Social Gospel of secular humanitarianism which included universal secular education, extension of the franchise, welfare measures, and the abolition of privilege.

More important but not unrelated to the question of the relative radicalism of the two wings of abolitionism is the question of their relative effectiveness. Until we can with some accuracy measure the impact of Garrisonian propaganda on the American mind, and until we have a systematic analysis of the Liberty party's effect on American politics at every level the question will go unanswered. In the meantime, we can, at least, ponder the role New York Liberty men played in the politics of their state and nation.

The great mission of the Liberty party was to make abolition of slavery the central theme of American politics. It was formed by those abolitionists who had become convinced that, unless injected into the political arena, antislavery agitation would fail. The abolitionists who recommended translating moral suasion into political action were not only motivated by the increasing possibility of electing antislavery congressmen in the 1840s but by the recognition that the evangelical revivalism of the 1820s and 1830s was burning itself out. To sustain the sincere moral abolitionist impulse, entrance into politics was thought necessary.

The initial goal of political action was to force politicians to make public their positions on issues related to slavery and the rights of the free Negro. Satisfactory responses would get abolitionist support; unsatisfactory answers would be matched by abolitionist opposition.[5]

New York election returns indicated that the abolitionists had vastly overrated the political strength of the movement. In 1838 in New York State the Whig gubernatorial candidate, William H. Seward, had answered questions evasively. The candidate for Lieutenant Governor, Luther Bradish, on the other hand, answered well enough to earn official endorsement by the abolitionists. Opponents of slavery were exhorted to vote for Bradish alone and thereby demonstrate the efficacy of the balance of power strategy. Seward and Bradish, however, were elected by almost exactly the same margin. In fact political abolitionism seems to have had some effect only in Oneida, Madison, and Lewis counties.[6]

Independent party machinery was thus thought necessary, the abolitionists hoping simultaneously to increase and demonstrate their vote-getting power. After the Liberty party began to run its own candidates slight gains were registered but "election results demonstrated that only a miniscule proportion of the voters felt strongly enough about abolitionism to support it at the polls."[7] The Liberty party vote in New York State went from 0.6 percent in 1840 to 1.6 percent in 1841, 1.8 percent in 1842, 4.5 percent in 1843, and declined to 3.1 percent in 1844.[8]

Despite this relatively low turnout, Liberty voting had effect in this era of extremely close political balance. While

[5] John Hendricks, "History of the Liberty Party in New York State" (Ph.D. diss., Fordham University, 1958), pp. 40 ff.

[6] Edwin Williams, *The New-York Annual Register for 1840, 1841, 1842, 1843, 1844* (New York: 1841–1845).

[7] Lee Benson, *The Concept of Jacksonian Democracy* (Princeton: Princeton University Press, 1961), p. 113.

[8] *Record of State Canvass,* 1828–1855, pp. 222–248, New York State Library, Manuscript Collection. Voting percentages, of course, do not measure the extent or effect of the political abolitionists' injection of the moral question into the arena of politics.

the Liberty percentage fell off substantially when statewide offices were at stake, local elections could push the major party groups in an area into antislavery positions. The impression one gets (this needs intense, systematic study) is that where the Liberty party was strongest in New York State, the Whigs became more of an antislavery party.

And despite the decline in 1844 to a 3.1 percent share of New York's votes for the Liberty party, abolitionist voting in that presidential year had a decisive and far-reaching effect. Liberty voters, the overwhelming majority of whom had voted Whig in 1840, provided a necessary and sufficient margin to deprive the Whig candidate, Henry Clay, of New York's thirty-six electoral votes, making James K. Polk President of the United States. Polk's expansionism was an important variable in the annexation of Texas and the Mexican War. The issues raised over the disquisition of lands acquired from Mexico as a result of the war intensified sectional tensions to such a degree as to make the Civil War a highly likely possibility.

While the war was not fought to free the slaves, it ultimately accomplished that. Slavery, like many other problems, could not be eliminated by piecemeal reform or through moral suasion alone. Southern leaders were aware that *any* tinkering was subversive and resisted it. The situation would not be resolved without violence. The nonresistance leader Garrison himself said that no oppressor class ever gives up its power and that the American slaveholders would be no exception. The political abolitionists, while rejecting a policy of overt violence, achieved an important result. They made clear the unwillingness of the South to accept any alteration of the institution of slavery.

But abolition, political or otherwise, had more than the destruction of the peculiar institution as its aim. Real freedom with political and economic equality for blacks was also a central concern. And ultimately, through direct political participation, too many Liberty leaders, in effect, sold out the blacks by deemphasizing the idea of racial equality in exchange for nonextension of slavery.

Liberty party men originally saw their political action as a mode of agitation that did not require a compromise of principle. The function was to awaken consciences and to disseminate truth. But ultimately their direct participation in politics encouraged many of them to emphasize more easily attainable results such as nonextension, at the cost of greater goals including a society based on brotherly love and racial equality.

Up to 1847 the Liberty party saw itself as a temporary vehicle of conversion for the old parties. The organization found it necessary and principled to keep to its "one-idea" approach and to support only its own candidates who were chosen from within the fold. By 1847, however, the strictness of Liberty action seemed in several places to be breaking down.[9]

At the National Convention of the Liberty party at Buffalo in October 1847, the antislavery leader John P. Hale, a former Democrat who had expressed a reluctance to affirm the constitutionality of abolition in the District of Columbia and prohibition of the interstate slave trade, received the presidential nomination over Gerrit Smith.[10] To be sure, the nomination met with opposition. Men such as William Goodell, James C. Jackson, Beriah Green, and especially James G. Birney denounced the choice. Birney believed that the party in "the nomination of Mr. Hale descended from the high and true principle which actuated it for many years."[11] Yet a

[9] Theodore Clarke Smith, *The Liberty and Free Soil Parties in the Northwest* (New York: Longmans, Green and Co., 1897), p. 114.

[10] Richard H. Sewell, *John P. Hale and the Politics of Abolition* (Cambridge: Harvard University Press, 1965), p. 90.

[11] James G. Birney to Lewis Tappan, 10 July 1848, Birney Papers, Library of Congress.

large number of New York abolitionists appear to have been ready to accept, even if without enthusiasm, leadership from one not originally of their number. This group was led by Lewis Tappan, Henry B. Stanton, and Joshua Leavitt.[12]

Even those who opposed outside nominations, however, began to urge departure from one-ideaism. Goodell, Green, Smith, Jackson, and Birney supported now the creation of a universal reform party—a party to act not as a temporary vehicle of conversion, but as a permanent political organization.[13] The list of reforms proposed added up to a remarkably Democratic kind of program, and thus it appears that these former Whigs were attempting, whether consciously or not, to broaden the base of their appeal.[14] The Liberty party was thus fractured by the nomination of an outsider, Hale, and by the secession of those who wished to expand the function of their political action.

The party was to be fractured again at the Free Soil Convention in 1848. The executive committee of the American and Foreign Anti-Slavery Society warned that the growing Free Soil movement was not truly an abolitionist movement: "Non-extension is not abolitionism although included in it, and it will be time to consider overtures of coalition from fellow citizens who have recently awakened to see the disastrous policy of slavery extension when they shall have embraced the great Anti-Slavery principles we avow." The committee also warned indirectly of the dangers of the Van Buren candidacy: "Neither can we believe that any Liberty party man will cast his vote for a politician who has, when in power, proffered his aid to the slaveocracy."[15]

12 Henry Brewster Stanton to John P. Hale, 6 July 1847, Hale Papers, New Hampshire Historical Society, Concord, N.H.

13 *Address of the Macedon Convention, By William Goodell and Letters of Gerrit Smith* (Albany: S. W. Green, 1847); Letter, Gerrit Smith to *Emancipator*, 23 August 1847.

14 Kraditor, *Means and Ends*, pp. 150–158.

15 *National Era*, 6 July 1848.

The names of two important New York State abolitionist leaders, William Jay and Alvan Stewart, were conspicuously missing from the signatures at the bottom of this warning. This was a signal of the coming process of coalition and co-optation many Liberty leaders would find themselves in. And at the Free Soil convention in Buffalo, most Liberty men approved the nomination of Martin Van Buren although some made no attempt to conceal their disappointment, and supported grudgingly or not at all the New Yorker's campaign.[16]

To Joshua Leavitt, it had seemed earlier that the Liberty party could not support Van Buren "without deliberately giving the lie to all our own declarations for fifteen years past."[17] With Henry Brewster Stanton, he traded away Hale's candidacy for Van Buren's in exchange for platform concessions and convinced other Liberty men to go along. All the platform concessions concerned the extension of slavery. There was no mention of abolition; but the glaring omission was the absence of a plank advocating equal rights for Negroes. Samuel R. Ward, the black abolitionist leader from New York, described the omission as a "studied and deliberate design" to avoid offending the Barnburner faction of the New York Democracy. While in most of the states outside New York, Free Soilers came from a tradition of support for Negro rights, the main organizational impulse in 1848 did come from the Barnburners of New York, and it was predictable that the Buffalo Free Soil platform would reflect their anti-Negro views.[18]

The party's platform was so broad as to gain support from

[16] Sewell, *John P. Hale,* pp. 100–108.

[17] Joshua Leavitt to Joshua Giddings, 6 July 1848, Giddings Papers, Ohio Historical Society, Columbus, Ohio.

[18] Eric Foner, "Politics and Prejudice: The Free Soil Party and the Negro, 1849–1852," *Journal of Negro History* 50 (October 1965): 239–256, and "Racial Attitudes of New York Free Soilers," *New York History* 46 (October 1965): 311–329.

the veteran abolitionist as well as from the most vulgar racist. Free Soil thus represented antislavery in its least radical form. Yet many Liberty men were willing to support it. Thus the "Free Soil party, in spite of the large admixture of Liberty men, was to adopt a fundamentally different policy from that adhered to by political abolitionists since 1840."[19] The Free Soil party was to give up the idea of Negro equality, and even appeal, when necessary, to Negrophobia, in order to broaden the base of antislavery. Once "the commitment to equal rights had been deleted from the platform of political anti-slavery, it would never again be reinserted."[20]

The Garrisonians were no doubt right in warning the Liberty men that they would be compromised by entering politics so directly. It is possible, however, that in order for the white mind and heart to have become convinced of Negro equality, whites would have to see substantial numbers of blacks outside the experience of slavery. If that is the case, the Liberty men, at least up to 1847, by forcing the moral question into politics did contribute significantly toward the accomplishment of that first step.[21]

In any case, it is not important for this particular study whether the abolitionist leaders were "right," either in their ends or their means. But I hope that the evidence presented in chapters 2, 3, and 4 suggests that they were not unusually frustrated people. The question of the validity of their arguments, objectives and means should continue to be a major area of investigation for historians. For it is too easy to dismiss the merits and arguments of social protest by "explaining away" that protest as a symptom of psychic conflict.

[19] Smith, *The Liberty and Free Soil Parties in the Northwest,* p. 159.
[20] Foner, "Racial Attitudes of New York Free Soilers," p. 326.
[21] It is possible that the movement gained more than it lost by the division of the moral suasionists and the Liberty men. Each wing "could pursue its aims independently, while antislavery sentiment grew year by year." See Wyatt-Brown, *Lewis Tappan.*

Appendix 1

New York's *100* Most Prominent Abolitionist Leaders

Anderson, Robert
Andrews, Josiah
Bailey, Wesley
Bancroft, Eleazer
Barkley, Thomas
Birney, James G.
Blair, Arba
Bouton, Nathan
Bradley, Henry
Brown, Abel
Campbell, Archibald
Chaplin, William L.
Childs, William H.
Clarke, E. W.
Corliss, Hiram
Cornish, Samuel E.
Cox, Abraham
Cox, Samuel H.
Culver, Erastus D.

Cuyler, Samuel
Delong, James C.
Denison, Charles W.
Downer, Joel G.
Edwards, John B.
Galusha, Elon
Garnet, Henry H.
Gates, Seth M.
Goodell, William
Goodwin, E. W.
Green, Beriah
Green, William R., Jr.
Hammond, Thomas H.
Hawley, C. M.
Hayt, Charles
Hicks, John F.
Holley, Myron
Hough, Reuben
Hough, Stanley

Hoyt, John C.
Jackson, James C.
Jay, William
Jocelyn, Simeon S.
Johnson, Thomas P.
Jonson, George W.
Kellogg, Spencer
Keyes, Perley G.
Knevels, John
Lawson, George
Leavitt, Joshua
Lee, Luther
Lewis, Melancton
Love, Thomas C.
McGregor, Alexander
Moore, Lindley Murray
Noble, Linnius P.
Orton, Philo A.
Palmer, D. B.
Parkhurst, Jabez
Phelps, Isaac
Pitts, Hiram
Plumb, Joseph
Plumb, Theron
Pritchett, E. C.
Putnam, Hiram
Rankin, John
Ray, Charles B.
Raymond, Asa
Ruggles, David
Savage, William H.

Seymour, Aseph
Shepard, Charles O.
Sherman, Henry
Sherman, Jarvis
Sims, James
Sleeper, Reuben
Smith, Gerrit
Smith, Horace E.
Smith, William R.
Snyder, Jacob
Sperry, Calvin
Stanford, John C.
Stanton, Henry B.
Stewart, Alvan
Stewart, Samuel
Sunderland, LaRoy
Tappan, Arthur
Tappan, Lewis
Thomas, John
Tucker, J. N. T.
Ward, Austin
Ward, Samuel R.
Warren, Asa
Wells, Samuel
Wetmore, Oliver
Wheaton, Charles A.
Wilkeson, Samuel, Jr.
Williams, Chauncey P.
Wilson, John I.
Wing, Asa
Wright, Theodore S.

Appendix 2

Summary of Findings in Michigan

Only six of twenty-one abolitionist leaders whose residence from 1840 to 1850 could be determined lived in small rural communities, while fifteen, or slightly more than 71 percent, resided during the decade of the 1840s in towns that were first or second in rank in their respective communities in both population and aggregate capital investment. And nine of these fifteen resided in Michigan's three largest manufacturing centers—Pontiac, Detroit, and Ann Arbor.

Manufacturers and merchants made up slightly more than 2 percent of Michigan's male workers, while within the ranks of Michigan's abolitionist leadership there were four merchants and manufacturers—or slightly more than 11 percent.

One and one-half percent of Michigan's working males followed the occupations of teacher, editor, doctor, lawyer, and clergyman, while 43 percent of the abolitionist leaders pursued these same callings. Twenty-three percent of the abolitionist leaders farmed for a living, and at the same time 60 percent of Michigan's general labor force were farmers.

All of the abolitionist leaders in Michigan held public office at

137

some time in their lives. Eleven of those whose pre-Liberty political affiliations I could determine were Whigs; none were Democrats. And for every year between 1825 and 1840, 22 percent of the thirty-seven leaders were officially engaged in public service.

The abolitionist leaders in fourteen of nineteen cases, or 74 percent, had vocations similar to those of their fathers, about whom there was a general lack of biographical information. The sons generally had more importance, influence, and economic affluence in their communities than their fathers had had in theirs.

Again, most important, the great majority of abolitionist leaders in Michigan were actively and intensely religious. Twenty-one of thirty-five were either pastors, deacons, or elders. Twenty-four of thirty-five abolitionist leaders, or slightly less than 69 percent, had been born and raised in New York or New England. In 1850, only 41 percent of Michiganders had been born in New York or New England. Moreover, eighteen of twenty-six, or slightly more than 69 percent of abolitionist leaders whose adult residences I could determine spent at least three years of their adult lives in New York (fifteen of eighteen) or New England (three of eighteen) during the period 1824–1833, the period of the Great Revival in these areas.

It appears that the Michigan abolitionist leader, like the New York abolitionist leader, was an urban, relatively prosperous, high-status citizen leading an "engaged" life. He resonated to abolitionism out of religious convictions which were reinforced during the era of revivalism.

Bibliography

Selected Secondary Works
on Antislavery and the Era of Reform

Abel, Annie H., and Klingberg, Frank J., eds. "A Sidelight on Anglo-American Relations, 1839–1861." *Journal of Negro History* 12 (1927): 128–329, 385–554.

Adams, Alice. *The Neglected Period of Anti-Slavery in America, 1808–1831.* Boston: Ginn & Co., 1908.

Aptheker, Herbert. "Militant Abolitionists." *Journal of Negro History* 26 (October 1941): 438–484.

———. "The Negro in the Abolitionist Movement." *Science and Society* 5 (1941): 2–23.

Barnes, Gilbert Hobbs. *The Anti-Slavery Impulse: 1830–1844.* New York: D. Appleton-Century Co., 1933.

Bartlett, Irving H. *Wendell Phillips, Brahmin Radical.* Boston: Beacon Press, 1961.

Basset, John Spencer. *Anti-Slavery Leaders in North Carolina.* Baltimore: Johns Hopkins University Press, 1898.

Bell, Howard H. "Expressions of Negro Militancy in the North, 1840–1860." *Journal of Negro History* 45 (January 1960): 11–20.

———. "National Negro Conventions of the Middle 1840's." *Journal of Negro History* 42 (October 1957): 55–70.

Bemis, Samuel. *John Quincy Adams and the Union.* New York: Alfred A. Knopf, 1956.

Benson, Lee. *The Concept of Jacksonian Democracy: New York as a Test Case.* Princeton: Princeton University Press, 1961.

Berwanger, Eugene. *The Frontier Against Slavery.* Urbana: University of Illinois Press, 1967.

Block, Muriel L. "Beriah Green the Reformer." Master's thesis, Syracuse University, 1935.

Boller, Paul F. "Washington, the Quakers, and Slavery." *Journal of Negro History* 46 (April 1961): 83–88.

Bretz, Julian P. "The Economic Background of the Liberty Party." *American Historical Review* 34 (January 1929): 250–264.

Brewer, W. M. "Henry Highland Garnet." *Journal of Negro History* 13 (January 1928): 36–52.

Brodie, Fawn M. *Thaddeus Stevens.* New York: W. W. Norton & Co., 1959.

Christian, H. N. "Samuel Cornish, Pioneer Negro Journalist." Master's thesis, Howard University, 1936.

Coburn, Frank W. "Joshua Leavitt." *Dictionary of American Biography.* Edited by Allen Johnson. Vol. 11. New York: Charles Scribner's Sons, 1933.

Cole, Charles C. *The Social Ideas of the Northern Evangelists, 1826–1860.* New York: Columbia University Press, 1954.

Commager, Henry Steele. *The Era of Reform, 1830–1860.* Princeton: Van Nostrand, 1960.

———. *Theodore Parker.* Boston: Houghton Mifflin, 1936.

Craven, Avery. *The Coming of the Civil War.* New York: Charles Scribner's Sons, 1942.

Crummel, Alexander. *Africa and America.* Springfield: Wiley and Co., 1891.

Current, Richard. *Old Thad Stevens.* Madison: University of Wisconsin Press, 1942.

Curry, Richard O. "Note on the Motives of Three Radical Republicans [with text of letters]." *Journal of Negro History* 47 (October 1962): 273–277.

Davis, David Brion. *The Problem of Slavery in Western Culture.* Ithaca: Cornell University Press, 1966.

————. "The Emergence of Immediatism in British and American Antislavery Thought." *Mississippi Valley Historical Review* 49 (September 1962): 209–230.

Demos, John. "The Anti-Slavery Movement and the Problem of Violent Means." *New England Quarterly* 37 (December 1964): 501–526.

Dillon, Merton L. *Elijah P. Lovejoy: Abolitionist Editor.* Urbana: University of Illinois Press, 1961.

————. "The Failure of American Abolitionists." *Journal of Southern History* 25 (May 1959): 159–177.

Donald, David. *Charles Sumner and the Coming of the Civil War.* New York: Alfred A. Knopf, 1960.

————. *Lincoln Reconsidered: Essays on the Civil War Era.* New York: Alfred A. Knopf, 1956.

————. "Reply" (to R. A. Skotheim, "Note on Historical Method"). *Journal of Southern History* 26 (February 1960): 156–157.

Drake, Thomas E. *Quakers and Slavery in America.* Yale Historical Publications Miscellany, no. 51. New Haven: Yale University Press, 1950.

Duberman, Martin B. "Abolitionists and Psychology." *Journal of Negro History* 47 (July 1962): 183–191.

————, ed. *Antislavery Vanguard.* Princeton: Princeton University Press, 1965.

————. *Charles Francis Adams.* Boston: Houghton Mifflin, 1961.

Dumond, Dwight Lowell. *Anti-Slavery: The Crusade for Freedom in America.* Ann Arbor: University of Michigan Press, 1961.

————. *Anti-Slavery Origins of the Civil War in the United States.* Ann Arbor: University of Michigan Press, 1939.

Ekirch, Arthur A. *The Idea of Progress in America, 1815–1860.* New York: Columbia University Press, 1944.

Elkins, Stanley M. *Slavery: A Problem in American Institutional and Intellectual Life.* Chicago: University of Chicago Press, 1959.

Farnam, Henry W. *Chapters in the History of Social Legislation in the United States to 1860.* Washington: Carnegie Institute, 1938.

Filler, Louis. *The Crusade Against Slavery, 1830–1860.* New York: Harper & Bros., 1960.

————. "Nonviolence and Abolition." *University Review* 30 (March 1964): 172–178.

Fladeland, Betty. *James Gillespie Birney: Slaveholder to Abolitionist.* Ithaca: Cornell University Press, 1955.

————. "Who Were the Abolitionists?" *Journal of Negro History* 49 (April 1964): 99–115.

Fletcher, Robert. *History of Oberlin College.* Vol. 1. Oberlin: Oberlin Press, 1943.

Foner, Eric. "Politics and Prejudice: The Free-Soil Party and the Negro, 1849–1852." *Journal of Negro History* 50 (October 1965): 239–256.

Fortenbaugh, Robert. "American Lutheran Synods and Slavery, 1830–1860." *Journal of Religion* 13 (1933): 72–92.

Fox, Early Lee. *American Colonization Society, 1817–1840.* Baltimore: Johns Hopkins University Press, 1919.

Franklin, John Hope. *From Slavery to Freedom: A History of American Negroes.* New York: Alfred A. Knopf, 1947.

Gara, Larry. *The Liberty Line: The Legend of the Underground Railroad.* Lexington: University of Kentucky Press, 1961.

————. "The Professional Fugitive in the Abolition Movement." *Wisconsin Magazine of History* (Spring, 1965): 196–204.

"Garnet, Henry Highland." *Appleton's Cyclopedia.* Edited by J. G. Wilson and John Fiske. Vol. 2. New York: D. Appleton and Co., 1888.

Garrison, Wendell Phillips, and Garrison, Francis Jackson. *William Lloyd Garrison: The Story of his Life told by his Children.* 4 vols. Boston: Houghton Mifflin Co., 1894.

Gatell, Frank O. "Doctor Palfrey Frees His Slaves." *New England Quarterly* 34 (March 1961): 74–86.

————. *John Gorham Palfrey and the New England Conscience.* Cambridge: Harvard University Press, 1963.

Greene, Lorenzo J. "Slaveholding New England and Its Awakening." *Journal of Negro History,* 13 (October 1928): 492–533.

Griffin, Clifford S. "The Abolitionists and the Benevolent Societies, 1831–1861." *Journal of Negro History* 44 (July 1959): 195–216.

————. *Their Brothers' Keepers: Moral Stewardship in the United States, 1800–1865.* New Brunswick: Rutgers University Press, 1960.

Gross, Bella. "Life and Times of Theodore S. Wright, 1797–1847." *Negro History Bulletin* 3 (June 1940): 133–138.

Hammond, Charles A. *Gerrit Smith: The Story of a Noble Life.* Geneva, New York: Press of W.F. Humphrey, 1908.

Harlow, Ralph V. "Gerrit Smith," *Dictionary of American Biography.* Edited by Allen Johnson. Vol. 17. New York: Charles Scribner's Sons, 1935.

———. *Gerrit Smith: Philanthropist and Reformer.* New York: Henry Holt & Co., 1939.

Hart, Albert Bushnell. *Slavery and Abolition, 1831–1841.* New York: Harper & Bros., 1906.

Harwood, Thomas F. "British Evangelical Abolitionism and American Churches in the 1830's." *Journal of Southern History* 28 (August 1962): 287–306.

Hirsch, Leo. "New York and the Negro from 1783 to 1865." *Journal of Negro History* 16 (October 1931): 415–487.

Hofstadter, Richard. *The Age of Reform.* New York: Alfred A. Knopf, 1955.

———. *American Political Tradition.* New York: Alfred A. Knopf, 1948.

Hume, John F. *The Abolitionists, Together with Personal Memories of the Struggle for Human Rights, 1830–1864.* New York: G. P. Putnam's Sons, 1905.

Jay, John. "William Jay," *Appleton's Cyclopedia.* Edited by J. G. Wilson and John Fiske. Vol. 3. New York: D. Appleton and Co., 1888.

Jenkins, W. S. *Pro-Slavery Thought in the Old South.* Chapel Hill: University of North Carolina Press, 1935.

Jonson, Oliver. *William Lloyd Garrison and his Times.* Boston: Houghton Mifflin, 1880.

Jordan, Winthrop. *White Over Black.* Chapel Hill: University of North Carolina Press, 1968.

Kearns, F. E. "Margaret Fuller and the Abolition Movement." *Journal of the History of Ideas* 25 (January 1964): 120–127.

Kerber, Linda K. "Abolitionists and Amalgamators: The New York City Race Riots of 1834." *New York History* 48 (January 1967): 28–40.

Kirkham, E. B. "Note on Two Abolitionists and a Pearl." *Journal of Negro History* 50 (April 1965): 123–125.

Klingberg, Frank Joseph. *The Anti-Slavery Movement in England.* New Haven: Yale University Press, 1926.

———. "Lewis Tappan," *Dictionary of American Biography.* Edited by Allen Johnson. Vol. 18. New York: Charles Scribner's Sons, 1936.

Korngold, Ralph. *Two Friends of Man: William Lloyd Garrison and Wendell Phillips.* Boston: Little, Brown & Co., 1950.

Kraditor, Aileen S. *Means and Ends in American Abolitionism.* New York: Pantheon, 1968.

Kraus, Michael. "Slavery Reform in the 18th Century: An Aspect of Trans-Atlantic Intellectual Cooperation." *Pennsylvania Magazine of History and Biography* 60 (1936): 53–66.

Lader, Lawrence. *The Bold Brahmins: New England's War Against Slavery, 1831–1863.* New York: E. P. Dutton & Co., Inc., 1961.

Landon, Fred. "Samuel Ringgold Ward." *Dictionary of American Biography.* Edited by Allen Johnson. Vol. 19. New York: D. Appleton and Co., 1936.

"Leavitt, Joshua," *Appleton's Cyclopedia.* Edited by J. G. Wilson and John Fiske. Vol. 3. New York: D. Appleton and Co., 1888.

Lerner, G. "Grimké Sisters and the Struggle Against Race Prejudice." *Journal of Negro History* 48 (October 1963): 277–291.

Lindsay, Arnett G. "Economic Conditions of the Negroes of New York prior to 1861." *Journal of Negro History* 6 (April 1921): 190–200.

Litwack, Leon F. "Abolitionist Dilemma: The Anti-Slavery Movement and the Northern Negro." *New England Quarterly* 24 (March 1961): 50–73.

———. *North of Slavery: The Negro in the Free States, 1790–1860.* Chicago: Chicago University Press, 1961.

Lloyd, Arthur Young. *The Slavery Controversy, 1831–1860.* Chapel Hill: University of North Carolina Press, 1939.

Locke, Mary Stoughton. *Anti-Slavery in America.* Boston: Ginn & Co., 1901.

Lofton, Williston H. "Abolition and Labor." *Journal of Negro History* 33 (July 1948): 249–283.

Loveland, Anne C. "Evangelicalism and 'Immediate Emancipation' in American Antislavery Thought." *Journal of Southern History* 32 (May 1966): 172–188.

Ludlum, Robert P. "Joshua Giddings, Radical." *Mississippi Valley Historical Review* 23 (June 1936): 49–60.

Lynd, Staughton. "Rethinking Slavery and Reconstruction." *Journal of Negro History* 50 (July 1965): 198–209.

MacDonald, William. "James Gillespie Birney." *Dictionary of American Biography*. Edited by Allen Johnson. Vol. 2. New York: Charles Scribner's Sons, 1929.

McMaster, John B. *The Acquisition of Political, Social and Industrial Rights of Man in America.* Cleveland: Imperial Press, 1903.

McPherson, James M. "Abolitionists and Negro Opposition to Colonization during the Civil War." *Phylon* 26 (Winter 1965): 391–399.

————. "Fight Against the Gag Rule: Joshua Leavitt and Anti-Slavery Insurgency in the Whig Party, 1839–1842." *Journal of Negro History* 48 (July 1963): 177–195.

Macy, Jesse. *The Anti-Slavery Crusade.* New Haven: Yale University Press, 1919.

Madison, Charles A. *Critics and Crusaders.* New York: Henry Holt & Co., 1947.

Mandel, Bernard, *Labor, Free and Slave: Workingmen and the Anti-slavery Movement in the United States.* New York: Associated Authors, 1955.

Martyn, Carlos. *Wendell Phillips: The Agitator.* New York: Funk and Wagnalls Co., 1890.

Mathews, Donald G. "Methodist Mission to the Slaves, 1829–1844." *Journal of American History* 51 (March 1965) 615–631.

Mathieson, William Law. *British Slavery and Its Abolition, 1823–1838.* London: Longmans, Green & Co., Ltd., 1926.

Maynard, Douglas H. "The World's Anti-Slavery Convention of 1840." *Mississippi Valley Historical Review* 47 (December 1960): 452–471.

Merrill, Walter M. *Against Wind and Tide: A Biography of William Lloyd Garrison.* Cambridge: Harvard University Press, 1963.

Milton, George F. *Eve of Conflict: Stephen A. Douglas and the Needless War*. New York: Houghton Mifflin, 1934.

Monaghan, Frank. "James Caleb Jackson." *Dictionary of American Biography*. Edited by Allen Johnson. Vol. 9. New York: Charles Scribner's Sons, 1932.

Nye, Russel B. *The Cultural Life of the New Nation*. New York: Harper & Row, 1960.

———. *Fettered Freedom*. East Lansing: Michigan State University Press, 1949.

———. "The Slave Power Conspiracy, 1830–1860." *Science and Society* 10 (Summer 1946): 262–274.

———. *William Lloyd Garrison and the Humanitarian Reformers*. Boston: Little Brown, 1955.

Pease, W. H. and Pease, Jane H. "Anti-slavery Ambivalence: Immediatism, Expediency, Race." *American Quarterly* 17 (Winter 1965): 682–695.

———, eds. *The Anti-slavery Argument*. New York: Bobbs-Merrill Co., 1965.

Peterson, A. E. "William Jay." *Dictionary of American Biography*. Edited by Allen Johnson. Vol. 10. New York: Charles Scribner's Sons, 1933.

Pickard, J. B. "John Greenleaf Whittier and the Abolitionist Schism of 1840." *New England Quarterly* 37 (June 1964): 250–254.

Pillsbury, Parker. *Acts of the Anti-slavery Apostles*. Concord, N.H.: Clague, Wegman Schlicht & Co., 1955.

Power, Richard L. "A Crusade to Extend Yankee Culture." *New England Quarterly* 13 (December 1940): 638–653.

Quarles, Benjamin. "Sources of Abolitionist Income." *Mississippi Valley Historical Review* 32 (June 1945): 63–87.

———. *Black Abolitionists*. New York: Oxford University Press, 1969.

Ratner, Lorman. "Northern Concern for Social Order as Cause for Rejecting Anti-Slavery, 1831–1840." *Historian* 28 (November 1965): 1–18.

———. "Northern Opposition to the Anti-Slavery Crusade, 1830–1840." Ph.D. dissertation, Cornell University, 1960.

———. *Powder Keg: Northern Opposition to the Antislavery Movement*. New York: Basic Books, 1968.

Rawley, J. A. "Joseph John Gurney's Mission to America, 1837–1840." *Mississippi Valley Historical Review* 49 (March 1963): 653–674.

Rayback, Joseph G. "The American Workingman and the Antislavery Crusade." *Journal of Economic History* 3 (1943): 152–163.

————. "The Liberty Party Leaders of Ohio: Exponents of Antislavery Coalition." *Ohio Archaeological and Historical Quarterly* 57 (1948): 165–178.

Rice, A. H. "Henry B. Stanton as a Political Abolitionist." Ph.D. dissertation, Columbia University, New York, 1968.

Rice, Madeleine Hooke. *American Catholic Opinion in the Slavery Controversy.* Columbia University Studies in History, Economics, and Public Law, no. 508. New York: Columbia University Press, 1944.

————. *Federal Street Pastor: The Life of William Ellery Channing.* New York: Bookman, 1961.

Riddleberger, Patrick W. "The Making of a Political Abolitionist: George W. Julian and the Free Soilers, 1848." *Indiana Magazine of History* 51 (1955): 222–236.

Robinson, Florence. "Reform Movements of the Thirties and Forties." Ph.D. dissertation, University of Wisconsin, 1925.

Russel, Robert Royal. *Ante Bellum Studies in Slavery, Politics and the Railroads.* Kalamazoo: Western Michigan University, 1960.

Schlesinger, Arthur M. *The American as Reformer.* Cambridge: Harvard University Press, 1950.

Schnell, Kempes. "Anti-Slavery Influence on the Status of Slaves in a Free State." *Journal of Negro History* 50 (October 1965): 257–273.

Sewell, Richard H. *John P. Hale and the Politics of Abolition.* Cambridge: Harvard University Press, 1965.

Shapiro, Samuel. *Richard Henry Dana, Jr.* East Lansing: Michigan State University Press, 1961.

Sherwin, Oscar. *Prophet of Liberty: The Life and Times of Wendell Phillips.* New York: Bookman Associates, 1956.

Siebert, Wilbur H. *The Underground Railroad.* 1892. Reprint. New York: Russel and Russel, 1967.

Sims, Henry H. *Emotion at High Tide: Abolition as a Controversial Factor, 1830–1845.* Richmond: William Byrd Press, 1960.

Skotheim, Robert A. "A Note on Historical Method: David Donald's 'Toward a Reconsideration of Abolitionists'." *Journal of Southern History* 25 (August 1959): 356–365.

Smith, Theodore Clarke. *The Liberty and Free Soil Parties in the Northwest*. Harvard Historical Studies, vol. 6. New York: Longmans, Green & Co., 1897.

————. *Parties and Slavery, 1850–1859*. New York: Harper & Bros., 1906.

Smith, Timothy L. *Revivalism and Social Reform in Mid-Nineteenth Century America*. Nashville, Tenn.: Abingdon Press, 1957.

Smith, William Henry. *A Political History of Slavery*. 2 vols. New York: G. P. Putnam's Sons, 1903.

Southall, Eugene P. "Arthur Tappan and the Anti-slavery Movement." *Journal of Negro History* 15 (April 1930): 162–198.

Stampp, Kenneth M. "Fate of Southern Anti-Slavery Sentiment." *Journal of Negro History* 28 (January 1943): 10–22.

"Stanton, Henry Brewster," *Appleton's Cyclopedia*. Edited by J. G. Wilson and John Fiske. Vol. 5. New York: D. Appleton & Co., 1888.

Stanton, William. *The Leopard's Spots: Scientific Attitudes toward Race in America, 1815–1859*. Chicago: University of Chicago Press, 1960.

Staudenraus, P. J. *The African Colonization Movement, 1816–1865*. New York: Columbia University Press, 1961.

Steiger, C. Bruce. "Abolitionism and the Presbyterian Schism of 1837–1838." *Mississippi Valley Historical Review* 36 (December 1949): 391–414.

Stewart, James B. "The Aims & Impact of Garrisonian Abolitionism, 1840–1860." *Civil War History* 15 (September 1969): 197–209.

Sweet, William. *Religion in the Development of American Culture*. New York: Charles Scribner's Sons, 1952.

Tannenbaum, Frank. *Slave and Citizen: The Negro in the Americas*. New York: Alfred A. Knopf, 1946.

Tanner, Edwin Platt. "Gerrit Smith, An Interpretation." *New-York Historical Society Quarterly* 5 (January 1924): 21–39.

Taylor, George. *The Transportation Revolution 1815–1860*. New York: Holt, Rinehart, and Winston, 1964.

Thistlethwaite, Frank. *The Anglo-American Connection.* Philadelphia: University of Pennsylvania Press, 1959.

Thomas, Benjamin Platt. *Theodore Weld, Crusader for Freedom.* New Brunswick: Rutgers University Press, 1950.

Thomas, John L. *The Liberator: William Lloyd Garrison.* Boston: Little, Brown & Co., 1963.

Tuckerman, Bayard. *William Jay and the Constitutional Movement for the Abolition of Slavery.* New York: Dodd, Mead and Co., 1893.

Tyler, Alice Felt. *Freedom's Ferment.* Minneapolis: University of Minnesota Press, 1944.

Van Deusen, Glyndon. *The Jacksonian Era.* New York: Harper & Bros., 1959.

Villard, Fanny Garrison. *William Lloyd Garrison on Nonresistance.* New York: The Nation Press, 1924.

Villard, Harold G. "Charles B. Ray." *Dictionary of American Biography.* Edited by Allen Johnson. Vol. 15. New York: Charles Scribner's Sons, 1935.

Villard, Oswald G. *John Brown.* Boston: Houghton Mifflin, 1950.

Waterman, W. Randall. "Beriah Green." *Dictionary of American Biography.* Edited by Allen Johnson. Vol. 7. New York: Charles Scribner's Sons, 1931.

———. "William Goodell." *Dictionary of American Biography.* Edited by Allen Johnson. Vol. 7. New York: Charles Scribner's Sons, 1931.

Weisberger, Bernard A. *They Gathered at the River: The Story of the Great Revivalists.* Boston: Little, Brown & Co., 1958.

Wesley, Charles H. "The Negro in Organization of Abolition." *Phylon* 2 (1941): 223–235.

———. "The Participation of Negroes in Antislavery Political Parties." *Journal of Negro History* 29 (January 1944): 32–74.

Wigham, Eliza. *The Anti-Slavery Cause in America and its Martyrs.* London: A. W. Bennett, 1863.

Williams, L. A. "Northern Intellectual Reaction to the Policy of Emancipation." *Journal of Negro History* 46 (July 1961): 174–188.

Williams, Mary W. "Henry Brewster Stanton." *Dictionary of Ameri-*

can Biography. Edited by Allen Johnson. Vol. 18. New York: Charles Scribner's Sons, 1936.

Wilson, Henry. *History of the Rise and Fall of the Slave Power in America.* 3 vols. Boston: James R. Osgood and Co., 1875.

Wolf, Hazel C. *On Freedom's Altar: The Martyr Complex in the Abolition Movement.* Madison: University of Wisconsin Press, 1952.

Woodson, Carter G. "Henry Highland Garnet." *Dictionary of American Biography.* Edited by Allen Johnson. Vol. 7. New York: Charles Scribner's Sons, 1931.

————, ed. *The Mind of the Negro as Reflected in Letters Written During the Crisis, 1800–1860.* Washington, D.C.: Associated Publishers, 1920.

————, ed. *Negro Orators and Their Orations.* Washington, D.C.: Associated Publishers, 1925.

Wyatt-Brown, Bertram. "Abolitionism: Its Meaning for Contemporary American Reform." *Midwest Quarterly* 8 (October 1966): 41–55.

————. "Abolitionists' Postal Campaign of 1835." *Journal of Negro History* 50 (October 1965): 227–238.

————. *Lewis Tappan & The Evangelical War Against Slavery.* Cleveland: Case Western Reserve University Press, 1969.

————. "William Lloyd Garrison and Antislavery Unity: A Reappraisal." *Civil War History* 13 (March 1967): 5–24.

Zorn, Roman J. "The New England Anti-Slavery Society: Pioneer Abolition Organization." *Journal of Negro History* 42 (July 1957): 157–176.

Selected Works on Social and Political Psychology

Allport, Gordon W. *Becoming: Basic Considerations for a Psychology of Personality.* New Haven: Yale University Press, 1955.

————. "The Trend in Motivational Theory." *American Journal of Orthopsychiatry* 23 (January 1953): 107–119.

Bell, Daniel, ed. *New American Right.* New York: Criterion Books, 1955.

Berkowitz, Leonard. *Aggression: A Social Psychological Analysis.* New York: McGraw-Hill Book Co., 1962.

Cantril, Hadley. *The Psychology of Social Movements.* New York: Wiley & Sons, Inc., 1941.

Cowley, W. S. "Three Distinctions in the Study of Leadership." *Journal of Abnormal and Social Psychology* 23 (Summer 1928): 144–157.

Crutchfield, Richard S. "Conformity and Character." *American Psychologist* 10 (May 1955): 191–198.

Duberman, Martin B. "The Abolitionists and Psychology." *Journal of Negro History* 47 (July 1962): 183–192.

Fromm, Erich. *The Dogma of Christ.* New York: Holt, Rinehart and Winston, 1963.

———. *The Sane Society.* New York: Holt, Rinehart and Winston, 1960.

Heberle, Rudolf. *Social Movements.* New York: Appleton-Century-Crofts, 1951.

Hinsie, Leland, and Campbell, Robert. *Psychiatric Dictionary.* New York: Oxford University Press, 1960.

Hyman, Herbert H. "The Psychology of Status." *Archives of Psychology,* No. 269 (1942).

Kelly, George. *The Psychology of Personal Constructs.* New York: W. W. Norton & Co., 1955.

Keniston, Kenneth. "Alienation and the Decline of Utopia." *American Scholar* 29 (1960): 161–211.

Lasswell, Harold. *Psychopathology and Politics.* Chicago: University of Chicago Press, 1930.

Lindzey, Gardner, ed. *Assessment of Human Motives.* New York: Holt, Rinehart and Winston, 1958.

Lundberg, George A. "Demographic and Economic Basis of Political Radicalism and Conservatism." *American Journal of Sociology* 32 (1927): 719–732.

McClosky, Herbert. "Conservatism and Personality." *American Political Science Review* 52 (March 1958): 27–45.

Mann, Arthur. "The Progressive Tradition." *Reconstruction of American History.* Edited by John Higham. New York: Harper & Bros., 1962.

Maslow, A. H. "Deprivation, Threat, and Frustration." C. L. Stacey and M. F. DeMartino, eds. *Understanding Human Motivation.* Cleveland: H. Allen, 1958.

Merton, Robert K. *Social Theory and Social Structure.* Glencoe: Free Press, 1957.

Paton, Stewart. "Psychology of the Radical." *Yale Review* 11 (October 1921): 89–101.

Rieff, Philip. *Freud: the Mind of the Moralist.* New York: Doubleday, 1961.

Rosenzweig, Saul. "An Outline of Frustration Theory." *Personality and Behavior Disorders.* Edited by J. McV. Hunt. New York: Ronald Press, 1944.

Scott, J. P. and Fredericson, Emil. "The Causes of Fighting in Mice and Rats." *Physiological Zoology* 24 (October 1951): 280–308.

Smith, M. Brewster. "Opinions, Personality and Political Behavior." *American Political Science Review* 52 (March 1958): 1–17.

————, Bruner, Jerome S., and White, Robert W. *Opinions and Personality.* New York: Wiley, 1956.

Tomkins, Silvan. *Affect, Cognition and Personality.* New York: Springer, 1965.

Woodward, C. Vann. "The Populist Heritage and the Intellectual." *American Scholar* 39 (Winter 1959): 56–73.

Wurtz, Kenneth R. "Some Theory & Data Concerning the Attenuation of Aggression." *Journal of Abnormal & Social Psychology* 60 (January 1960): 134–136.

Contemporary Works

American Anti-Slavery Society. *Address to the People of Color in the City of New York, by Members of the Executive Committee of the American Anti-Slavery Society.* New York: S. W. Benedict, 1834.

————. *First Annual Report of the American Anti-Slavery Society.* New York: Dorr and Butterfield, 1834.

————. *Second Annual Report of the American Anti-Slavery Society.* New York: William S. Dorr, 1835.

————. *Third Annual Report of the American Anti-Slavery Society.* New York: William S. Dorr, 1836.

————. *Fourth Annual Report of the American Anti-Slavery Society.* New York: William S. Dorr, 1837.

————. *Fifth Annual Report of the American Anti-Slavery Society.* New York: William S. Dorr, 1838.

————. *Sixth Annual Report of the Executive Committee of the American Anti-Slavery Society.* New York: William S. Dorr, 1839.

————. *Seventh Annual Report of the Executive Committee of the American Anti-Slavery Society.* New York: William S. Dorr, 1840.

————. *A Collection of Valuable Documents, Being Birney's Vindication of Abolitionists—Protest of the American Anti-Slavery Society—To the People of the United States, or, To Such Americans as Value Their Rights—Letter from the Executive Committee of the New York Anti-Slavery Society to the Executive Committee of the Ohio State Anti-Slavery Society at Cincinnati—Outrage upon Southern Rights.* Boston: Isaac Knapp, 1836.

————. *The Declaration of Sentiments and Constitution of the American Anti-Slavery Society. Together with All Those Parts of the Constitution of the United States Which Have Relation to Slavery.* New York: American Anti-Slavery Society, 1835.

Birney, James G. *The American Churches: The Bulwarks of American Slavery.* Newburyport: C. Whipple, 1842.

————. *Correspondence Between the Hon. F. H. Elmore, One of the South Carolina Delegation in Congress, and James G. Birney, One of the Secretaries of the American Anti-Slavery Society.* New York: American Anti-Slavery Society, 1838.

————. *Letter on Colonization, Addressed to the Rev. Thornton J. Mills, Corresponding Secretary of the Kentucky Colonization Society.* New York: American Anti-Slavery Reporter, 1834.

————. *A Letter on the Political Obligations of Abolitionists, with a Reply by William Lloyd Garrison.* Boston: Dow and Jackson, 1845.

Birney, William. *James G. Birney and His Times.* New York: D. Appleton & Co., 1890.

Broadway Tabernacle Anti-Slavery Society. *Proceedings of a Meeting to Form the Broadway Tabernacle Anti-Slavery Society, with the Constitution, etc., and Address to the Church.* New York: William S. Dorr, 1838.

Clay, Cassius M. *A Letter of Cassius M. Clay to the Mayor of Day-*

ton, Ohio, with a Review of it by Gerrit Smith. [Utica] Jackson
and Chaplin [1844].

[Colton, Calvin.] "Political Abolition." *The Junius Tracts.* No. 5.
New York: Greeley and McElroth, 1844.

Cornish, Samuel E. *The Colonization Movement Considered.* Newark: A. Guest, 1840.

Cox, Samuel H. *Correspondence between S. H. Cox and Frederick Douglass.* New York: American Anti-Slavery Society, 1846.

Davis, W. *The Liberty Party Practicable and It Will Be Successful.* n.p., n.d.

Douglass, Frederick. *The Anti-Slavery Movement.* Rochester: Lee Mann and Co., 1855.

————. *Life and Times of Frederick Douglass written by himself.* Century Memorial Subscriber edition. New York: Pathway Press, 1941.

[Dunlop, John.] *American Anti-Slavery Conventions: A Series of Extracts Illustrative of the Proceedings and Principles of the "Liberty Party" in the United States, with the Bearing of the Anti-Slavery Cause on Missions.* Edinburgh: William Oliphant and Sons, 1846.

Emancipator Extra: The Right Sort of Politics. Easton, 1843.

An Examination of Mr. Bradish's answer to the Interrogatories Presented to him by a Committee of the State Anti-Slavery Society. Albany: Hoffman and White, 1838.

Female Anti-Slavery Society of Chatham Street Chapel. *Constitution and Address of the Female Anti-Slavery Society of Chatham Street Chapel.* New York: William S. Dorr, 1834.

Friends, New York Yearly Meeting. *An Address of Friends of New York to the Citizens of the United States.* New York: Mahlon, Day and Co., 1844.

————. *Address to the Citizens of the United States of America on the Subject of Slavery, from the Yearly Meeting of the Religious Society of Friends (called Quakers), Held in New York.* New York: Mahlon Day, 1837.

Garnet, Henry Highland. *A Memorial Discourse.* Philadelphia: J. M. Wilson, 1865.

Garrison, William Lloyd. *Principles and Mode of Action of the*

American Anti-Slavery Society. Leeds Antislavery Series No. 86. London: William Tweedie, 1853.

Goodell, Lavinia. *In Memoriam, William Goodell, Born in Coventry, New York, October 25, 1792. Died in Janesville, Wisconsin, February 14, 1878.* Chicago: Gilbert & Winchell, 1879.

Goodell, William. *Address of the Macedon Convention by William Goodell and Letters of Gerrit Smith.* Albany: S. W. Green, 1847.

——. *Come-Outerism: The Duty of Secession from a Corrupt Church.* New York: American Anti-Slavery Society, 1845.

——. *Slavery and Anti-Slavery: A History of the Great Struggle in Both Hemispheres, with a View of the Slavery Question in the United States.* New York: William Harned, 1852.

——. *Views of American Constitutional Law in its Bearing upon American Slavery.* Utica: Jackson and Chaplin, 1844.

Green, Beriah. *The Chattel Principle and Abhorrence of Jesus Christ and the Apostles: or, No Refuge for American Slavery in the New Testament.* New York: American Anti-Slavery Society, 1839.

——. *Four Sermons.* Cleveland: Herald Office, 1833.

——. "A Letter to a Minister of the Gospel." *Quarterly Anti-Slavery Magazine* 1 (July 1836): 338–339.

——. *The Martyr: a Discourse in Commemoration of the Martyrdom of the Rev. Elijah P. Lovejoy, Delivered in Broadway Tabernacle, New York; and in the Bleecker Street Church, Utica.* New York: American Anti-Slavery Society, 1838.

——. *Miscellaneous Writings.* Whitesboro: Oneida Institute, 1841.

——. *Sketches of the Life and Writings of James Gillespie Birney.* Utica: Jackson and Chaplin, 1844.

——. *Things for Northern Men To Do.* Whitesboro: Oneida Institute, 1836.

Holley, Myron. *An Address Delivered at Perry, New York, July 4, 1839.* Perry, N.Y.: Mitchell & Warren, 1839.

Holley, Sallie. *A Life for Liberty; Anti-slavery and Other Letters of Sallie Holley.* Edited by John W. Chadwick. New York: G. P. Putnam's Sons, 1905.

Jay, William. *An Inquiry into the Character and Tendency of the*

American Colonization and American Anti-Slavery Societies. New York: Leavitt, Lord & Co., 1835.

————. *Miscellaneous Writings on Slavery.* Boston: J. P. Jewett, 1853.

————. *A View of the Action of the Federal Government in Behalf of Slavery.* New York: J. S. Taylor, 1839.

Ladies' New York City Anti-Slavery Society. *First Annual Report of the Ladies' New York Anti-Slavery Society.* New York: William S. Dorr, 1836.

Lewis County Anti-Slavery Society. *Sketch of Proceedings of the Lewis County Anti-Slavery Society, Convened in the Village of Lowville, January 10, 1837.* Watertown: Knowlton & Rice, 1837.

Liberty Tracts. Utica: Jackson and Chaplin, 1844.

May, Samuel J. *Some Recollections of the Anti-Slavery Conflict.* Boston: Field, Osgood & Co., 1869.

Minutes of the Christian Anti-Slavery Convention Assembled April 17th–20th, 1850. Cincinnati, 1850.

Minutes of the 1833 Convention of Free People of Color. Philadelphia, 1833.

Minutes of the National Convention of Colored Citizens held at Buffalo, New York, on the 15th, 16th, 17th, 18th, and 19th of August 1843, for the Purpose of Considering Their Moral and Political Conditions as American Citizens. New York: Princy and Reed, 1843.

New York City Anti-Slavery Society. *Address of the New York City Anti-Slavery Society to the People of the City of New York.* New York: West and Trow, 1833.

New York Committee of Vigilance. *The First Annual Report of the New York Committee of Vigilance, for the year 1837, together with Important Facts Relative to their Proceedings.* New York: Piercy and Reed, 1837.

New York State Anti-Slavery Society. *A Letter from the Executive Committee of the New York Anti-Slavery Society to the Executive Committee of the Ohio State Anti-Slavery Society at Cincinnati.* Utica: New York State Anti-Slavery Society, 1836.

————. *Proceedings of the First Annual Meeting of the New York*

State Anti-Slavery Society Convened at Utica, October 19, 1836.
Utica: New York State Anti-Slavery Society, 1836.

———. *Proceedings of the New York Anti-Slavery Convention, held at Utica, October 21, and New York State Anti-Slavery Society, held at Peterboro, October 22, 1835.* Utica: Standard and Democrat, 1835.

New York Young Men's Anti-Slavery Society. *Address of the New York Young Men's Anti-Slavery Society, to their Fellow Citizens.* New York: W. T. Coolidge & Co., 1834.

———. *First Annual Report of the New York Young Men's Anti-Slavery Society, Auxiliary to the American Anti-Slavery Society; with Addresses, delivered at the Anniversary, May 1835.* New York: Coolidge & Lambert, 1835.

———. *Preamble and Constitution of the New York Young Men's Anti-Slavery Society, formed May 2, 1834.* New York: W. T. Coolidge & Co., 1834.

Proceedings and Address of the [1841] Liberty National Nominating Convention. n.p., n.d.

Proceedings of the National Liberty Convention, Held at Buffalo, June 14th, and 15th, 1848, including the Resolutions and Addresses Adopted by That Body, and Speeches by Beriah Green on That Occasion. Utica: S. W. Green, 1848.

Ray, Florence T. *Sketch of the Life of Charles B. Ray.* New York: J. J. Little & Co., 1887.

Report of the New York State Vigilance Committee, 1853. New York, 1853.

Smith, Gerrit. *Constitutional Argument Against Slavery.* Utica: Jackson and Chaplin, 1844.

———. *Reply to the Colored Citizens of Albany.* Peterboro: n.p., 1848.

———. *Report from the County of Madison.* Peterboro: n.p., 1843.

———. *Sermons and Speeches of Gerrit Smith.* New York: Ross and Tousey, 1861.

———. *Speech of Gerrit Smith, made in the National Convention of the Liberty Party, at Buffalo, October 21, 1847, on the Character, Scope, and Duties of the Liberty Party.* Albany: S. W. Green, 1847.

————. *To the Friends of the Slave in the Town of Smithfield.* Peterboro: n.p., 1844.

Stanton, Henry Brewster. *Random Recollections.* Johnstown, N.Y.: Blunck and Leaning, 1885.

Stewart, Alvan. *Slavery in New Jersey: Legal Argument before the Supreme Court of the State of New Jersey, at the May Term, 1848, at Trenton, for the Deliverance of four thousand Persons from Bondage.* New York: Finch and Week, 1845.

————. *Writings and Speeches of Alvan Stewart on Slavery.* Edited by Luther Rawson March. New York: A. B. Burdick, 1860.

Sunderland, LaRoy. *Anti-Slavery Manual.* New York: S. W. Benedict, 1837.

Tappan, Lewis. *Address to the Non-Slaveholders of the South.* New York: n.p., 1843.

————. *The Life of Arthur Tappan.* New York: Hurd and Houghton, 1870.

————. *A Sidelight on Anglo-American Relations, 1839–1858, furnished by the correspondence of Lewis Tappan and others with the British and Foreign Anti-Slavery Society.* Edited by Annie H. Abel and Frank J. Klingberg. Lancaster, Pa.: Association for the Study of Negro Life and History, 1927.

Ward, Samuel Ringgold. *Autobiography of a Fugitive Negro.* London: J. Snow Publishers, 1855.

Wright, Elizur. *Myron Holley and What He Did for Liberty and True Religion.* Boston: Elizur Wright, 1882.

Manuscript Materials

Birney Papers. *Letters and Papers of James Gillespie Birney.* William L. Clements Library, University of Michigan, Ann Arbor, Michigan. The letters in this collection related to the antislavery movement are published in Dwight L. Dumond, ed. *Letters of James Gillespie Birney, 1831–1857.* 2 vols. New York: D. Appleton-Century, 1838.

Letters and Papers of James Gillespie Birney. Library of Congress, Manuscript Division.

Miscellaneous Manuscripts, James G. Birney, New-York Historical Society.

Letters of Notables in Gerrit Smith Miller Collection, Syracuse University Manuscript Division.

Bradish, Luther. *Letters.* New-York Historical Society.

Clarke, E. W. *Diary.* New York State Historical Association, Cooperstown, New York.

Goodell Papers. *Letters and Papers of William Goodell.* Berea College Library, Berea, Kentucky.

Hale, John P. *Papers.* New Hampshire Historical Society.

Holley, Myron. *Miscellaneous Manuscripts.* New-York Historical Society.

May, Samuel J. *Antislavery Collection.* Cornell University Library, Ithaca, New York.

Minutes of the New York State Liberty Party Convention, January 19 and 20, 1842. New-York Historical Society.

Minutes of the Proceedings of the Executive Committee of the Dutchess County Anti-Slavery Society, from May 29, 1838 to May 11, 1840. Manuscript Division, New York Public Library.

Noble, L. P. *Miscellaneous Manuscripts.* New-York Historical Society.

O'Reilly, Henry. *Collection.* Rochester Historical Society, Rochester, New York.

Sleeper, Reuben. Papers in *Porter Collection.* Old Fort Niagara Association, Youngstown, New York.

Slavery Manuscripts. New-York Historical Society.

Smith Papers. *Letters and Papers of Gerrit Smith.* The most comprehensive collection is in the Syracuse University Library, Syracuse, New York. It includes copybook of what appears to be every letter Smith wrote and collections of letters from Birney, Chaplin, Clarke, Cornish, S. Cox, Garnet, Gates, Goodell, B. Green, Holley, R. S. Hough, Jackson, Jay, Jocelyn, Jonson, Leavitt, Ray, Ruggles, Stanton, Stewart, A. and L. Tappan, Thomas, Ward, Wright.

Many of the letters in that collection which were addressed to Smith are listed in *Calendar of the Gerrit Smith Papers in the Syracuse University Library, 1819–1854.* 2 vols. Syracuse: Historical Records Survey, 1941.

Other Smith letters are in the New York Public Library, the

New-York Historical Society Library, and the Madison County Historical Society in Oneida, New York.

Stewart Papers. *Letters and Papers of Alvan Stewart.* The two largest collections are in the New York State Historical Association Library, Cooperstown, New York and the New-York Historical Society Library, New York.

Treadwell, Seymour B. *Papers, 1818–1869,* containing letters from Gerrit Smith, Alvan Stewart. William L. Clements Library, Ann Arbor.

Weld, Theodore Dwight. *Miscellaneous Letters from Beriah Green, Gerrit Smith, Wendell Phillips, et. al., Respecting Anti-Slavery Matters.* Library of Congress, Washington, D.C.

Weld-Grimké Papers. *Letters and Papers of Theodore Dwight Weld, Angelina Grimké Weld, and Sarah Grimké.* William L. Clements Library, University of Michigan, Ann Arbor.

The letters in this collection relating to the antislavery movement are published in Gilbert H. Barnes and Dwight L. Dumond, eds., *Letters of Theodore Dwight Weld, Angelina Grimké Weld, and Sarah Grimké, 1822–1844.* 2 vols. New York: Appleton-Century, 1934.

Newspapers

Albany Argus.

Albany Patriot.

The Christian Investigator. Whitesboro, New York.

Colored American. New York.

Emancipator. New York and Boston.

Friend of Man. Utica.

Herald of Freedom. Keeseville, New York.

Liberator. Boston.

Liberty Press. Utica.

National Anti-Slavery Standard. New York.

New York Ballot Box.

New York Herald.

New York Tribune.
Skaneateles Communitist.
Tocsin of Liberty. Albany.

Documents

New York State. *Census of 1855.* Albany: Charles Van Bent Huysen, 1857.

New York State Register for 1843, containing an almanac, civil divisions, and a census of the state, with political, statistical and other information, relating to the State of New York and the United States, also a full list of county officers, attorneys, etc. Albany: J. Disturnell, 1843. See also *Supplements* for 1844, 1846, and 1847.

Record of State Canvass, 1828–1855. New York State Library, Manuscript Collection.

United States Bureau of the Census. *Negroes in the United States.* Washington: Government Printing Office, 1935.

United States, *Census of 1850.* Washington: A. O. P. Nicholson, 1854.

Williams, Edwin, ed. *The New York Annual Register for the Year of Our Lord 184[0–45].* New York: Turner and Haydon, 1845.

Works Dealing Primarily
with New York State

Alexander, De Alva Stanwood. *A Political History of the State of New York.* 6 vols. New York: Henry Holt, 1906.

Anderson, G. B. *Landmarks of Rensselaer County.* Syracuse: D. Mason and Co., 1897.

Bagg, M. M. *Memorial History of Utica, New York.* Syracuse: D. Mason, 1892.

Bailey, William S. "Underground Railroad in Southern Chautauqua County." *New York History* 33 (January 1935), 53–63.

Beardsley, Levi. *Reminiscences of Otsego.* New York: n.p., 1852.

Beers, F. W. *Gazeteer and Biographical Record of Genesee County, New York: 1888–1890.* Syracuse: J. W. Vose and Co., 1890.

————. *Wyoming County.* New York: F. W. Beers, 1880.

Bungay, G. W. *Pen and Ink Portraits.* Albany: J. Munsell, 1857.

Chautauqua History Company, comp. *Centennial History of Chautauqua County.* Jamestown, New York: Chautauqua History Company, 1904.

Cleveland, S. G. *Yates County.* Penn Yan, New York: n.p., 1873.

Cole, Charles C., Jr. "The Free Church Movement in New York City." *New York History* 34 (July 1953): 284–297.

————. "The New Lebanon Convention." *New York History* 31 (October 1950): 385–397.

Coles, Howard W. *The Cradle of Freedom: A History of the Negro in Rochester, Western New York and Canada.* Rochester: Oxford Press, 1943.

Cookingham, Henry J. *History of Oneida County.* Chicago: S. J. Clarke, 1912.

Cross, Whitney R. *The Burned-Over District: The Social and Intellectual History of Enthusiastic Religion in Western New York, 1800–1850.* Ithaca: Cornell University Press, 1950.

Dorn, Adelaide Elizabeth, "A History of the Anti-Slavery Movement in Rochester and Vicinity." Master's thesis, University of Buffalo, 1932.

Douglass, Harry. *Progress With a Past.* Arcade, New York: Arcade Sesquicentennial and Historical Society, 1957.

Dyson, Zita. "Gerrit Smith's Effort in Behalf of the Negroes in New York." *Journal of Negro History* 3 (October 1918): 354–359.

Ellis, David M., Frost, James A., and Syrett, Harold. *A Short History of New York State.* Ithaca: Cornell University Press, 1957.

Ellis, Walter J. "Editorial Attitudes of the *Onondaga Standard* on Slavery from 1829–1848." Master's thesis, Syracuse University, 1942.

Ellithorpe, Susan J. "Early Development of the Anti-Slavery Crusade with Special Reference to New York." Master's thesis, Syracuse University, 1934.

Everest, Allan S. *Recollections of Clinton County.* Plattsburgh: Clinton County Historical Society, 1964.

Everts, L. H. *History of Jefferson County.* Philadelphia: Everts, 1878.

Foner, Eric. "Racial Attitudes of the New York Free Soilers." *New York History* 46 (October 1965): 311–329.

Fox, Dixon Ryan. *Yankees and Yorkers.* New York: New York University Press, 1940.

Frothingham, Octavius Brooks. *Gerrit Smith, a Biography.* New York: G. P. Putnam's Sons, 1878.

Frothingham, Washington. *History of Fulton County.* Syracuse: D. Mason and Co., 1892.

Gallwey, Sydney. *Peter Webb, Slave–Freeman–Citizen of Tompkins County, New York.* Ithaca: De Witt Historical Society of Tompkins County, Inc., 1960.

Genung, Elizabeth. *West Hill and Some of its Historic Homes and Families.* Ithaca: De Witt Historical Society, 1964.

Goodwin, H. C. *Pioneer History of Cortland County.* New York: Burdick, 1859.

Graf, Hildegarde Francis. "Abolition and Antislavery in Buffalo and Erie County." Master's thesis, University of Buffalo, 1939.

Hammond, L. M. *History of Madison County.* Syracuse: Truair, Smith and Co., 1872.

Hanmer-Croughton, Amy. "Anti-slavery Days in Rochester." *Rochester Historical Society Publication Fund Series,* 14 (1936): 113–155.

Hardin, G. A., and Willard, F. H. *History of Herkimer County.* Syracuse: D. Mason and Co., 1893.

Harlow, Ralph Volney. "Gerrit Smith and the Free Church Movement." *New York History* 18 (July 1937): 269–287.

Henderson, Alice H. "The History of the New York State Anti-Slavery Society." Ph.D. dissertation, University of Michigan, 1963.

Hendricks, John R. "History of the Liberty Party in New York State, 1838–1848." Ph.D. dissertation, Fordham University, New York, 1958.

History of Niagara County, New York. New York: Sanford and Co., 1878.

Johnson, Crisfield. *Centennial History of Erie County, New York.* Buffalo: Matthews and Warren, 1876.

Loucks, Esther C. "The Anti-Slavery Movement in Syracuse from 1839–1858." Master's thesis, Syracuse University, 1934.

McIntosh, W. H. *Monroe County*. Philadelphia: Everts, 1877.

———. *Wayne County*. Philadelphia: Everts, 1877.

McMahon, Helen G. *Chautauqua County: A History*. Buffalo: Henry Stewart, 1958.

McManus, Edgar J. "Antislavery legislation in New York." *Journal of Negro History* 46 (October 1961): 208–216.

Merrill, Arch. *Pioneer Profiles*. New York: American Book-Stratford Press, Inc., 1957.

Millikin, Charles F. *Ontario County*. New York: Lewis Historical Publishing Co., 1911.

Moseley, T. R. "A History of The New York Manumission Society, 1785–1849." Ph.D. dissertation, New York University, 1963.

Myers, John. "The Beginning of Antislavery Agencies in New York State, 1833–1836." *New York History* (April 1962): 149–181.

Northrup, Ansel Judd. *Slavery in New York: A Historical Sketch*. Albany: University of the State of New York, 1900.

Parker, Amasa J. *Landmarks of Albany County*. Syracuse: D. Mason, 1897.

Plunkett, Margaret L. "A History of the Liberty Party with Emphasis upon its Activities in the Northeastern States." Ph.D. dissertation, Cornell University, 1930.

Proctor, L. B. *Bench and Bar of New York*. New York: Diossy and Co., 1870.

Roach, George W. "The Presidential Campaign of 1844 in New York State." New York History 19 (April 1938): 153–172.

Roberts, Millard F. *History of Remsen*. New York: M. F. Roberts, 1914.

Scisco, Louis Dow. *Political Nativism in New York State*. Studies in History, Economics and Public Law, edited by the Faculty of Political Science of Columbia University, vol. 13, no. 2. New York: Columbia University Press, 1901.

Seifman, E. "A History of the New-York State Colonization Society." Ph.D. dissertation, New York University, 1965.

Signor, Isaac S. *Landmarks of Orleans County*. Syracuse: D. Mason, 1894.

Smith, Charles Carroll. *Pioneer Times in the Onondaga Country.* Syracuse: C. W. Bardeen, 1904.

Smith, H. Perry. *History of the City of Buffalo and Erie County.* Vol. 1. Syracuse: D. Mason and Co., 1884.

Smith, James H. *The History of Livingston County.* Syracuse: D. Mason and Co., 1881.

Smith, John. *Descriptive and Biographical Record of Madison County.* Boston: Boston Historical Co., 1899.

Storke, Elliot G. *History of Cayuga County.* Syracuse: D. Mason, 1879.

Sylvester, N. B. *Saratoga County.* Philadelphia: Everts and Ensign, 1878.

Thomas, Arad. *Pioneer History of Orleans County.* Albion, New York: H. A. Bruner, 1871.

Ver Nooy, Amy Pearce. "The Anti-Slavery Movement in Dutchess County, 1835–1850." *Year Book, Dutchess County Historical Society* 28 (1943): 57–66.

Vigilante, Emil C. "The Temperance Reform in New York State, 1829–1851." Ph.D. dissertation, New York University, 1964.

Wager, Daniel E. *Our County and its People; A Descriptive Work on Oneida County.* Boston: Boston Historical Co., 1896.

————. *The City of Rome.* Boston: Boston Historical Co., 1896.

Wesley, Charles Harris. "The Negroes of New York in the Emancipation Movement." *Journal of Negro History* 24 (January 1939): 65–103.

White, Truman C. *Our County and Its People: A Descriptive Work on Erie County, New York.* 2 vols. Boston: Boston Historical Co., 1898.

Yoshpe, Henry. "Record of Slave Manumissions in Albany, 1800–1828." *Journal of Negro History* 26 (October 1941): 499–521.

Young, A. M. *History of Chautauqua County.* Buffalo: Matthews and Wanes, 1875.

Werner, E. A. *Civil List of New York.* Albany: Weed, Parsons and Co., 1888.

Index

The New York Abolitionists was composed
in Linotype Baskerville, with Bulmer display type,
by The Book Press, Brattleboro, Vermont.
The entire book was printed
by letterpress.